LEEDS UNIT]
LIFE IN THE PRESS BOX

A journalist for more than 40 years, mostly covering sport, John Wray was born in Bramley, Leeds, in 1946 and has known every Leeds United manager from Don Revie to Gary McAllister.

Having attended Allerton Grange School as a 'guinea pig' for comprehensive education, he gained his A-level GCEs before training on the *Pudsey and Stanningley News* where he was Sports Editor and eventually Deputy Editor. From there he moved to Bradford's evening paper, the *Telegraph & Argus*, as a news reporter, though he quickly switched to full time sports reporting, becoming the paper's Leeds United writer for 20 years.

Travelling throughout this country and Europe with the Leeds team, he became a close friend to many of the players and backroom staff, receiving a privileged insight into their lives and going on to edit the club's match-day programme.

After sub-editing as a 'casual' in the Manchester offices of the *Daily Mail* and *Daily Express* to gain experience and earn extra cash—not necessarily in that order—John entered full time freelancing by joining the Leeds-based Gosnay's Sports Agency in 1990 and is a partner in the business.

When Elland Road was chosen as one of the venues for Euro 96, he was seconded to the Football Association for over a year, publicising the tournament as the FA's Yorkshire area press officer, which included making numerous appearances on TV and radio.

In 2005, John researched and co-wrote *Where Are They Now—Life After Leeds United*, a fascinating book revealing the occupations and whereabouts of a host of Leeds players from the Revie era onwards.

Married to former professional ice-skater Helen Leaman, John has two grown-up daughters, Liz and Louise, and grandsons Oliver and Harry.

LEEDS UNITED AND A LIFE IN THE PRESS BOX

JOHN WRAY

VERTICAL EDITIONS

www.verticaleditions.com

First published in the United Kingdom in 2008 by
Vertical Editions, Unit 4a, Snaygill Industrial Estate,
Skipton, North Yorkshire BD23 2QR

www.verticaleditions.com

ISBN 978-1-904091-32-5

Cover design and typeset by HBA, York

Printed and bound by Biddles, King's Lynn

This book is dedicated to my long suffering wife Helen and daughters Liz and Louise for all those times I was away with Leeds United and missed being at home with them. The life of a sports journalist can be so anti-social.

CONTENTS

FOREWORD

When John asked me to write a foreword for his book I was delighted because it revived many happy memories of our trips to away grounds at home and abroad on the Leeds United team coach.

They were different times when the press lads were allowed on the coach and managers had sufficient confidence in the guys to allow them to travel with us. For matches in Europe, writers from the national papers joined us too, but for most domestic trips it was the local lads like John who came along and were almost part of the squad!

They were enjoyable times. The press lads used to ring us up for a chat and we knew they would never misinterpret what we said when we read it in the papers. Nowadays, to a larger extent, the press are under more pressure to find juicy stories and the kind of headlines that sell papers.

Unfortunately, good news isn't treated as real news anymore and if newspapers had been run in my playing days the way they are today, pressmen wouldn't have been allowed on the bus. I have seen how the media works from both sides of the spectrum—as a player and in my role as a local newspaper columnist and an occasional radio broadcaster. It's a different approach when working for local media rather than national organisations because there's a tendency to be a little more understanding and sympathetic when covering the local club.

It was much easier in the early days for the journos to get their story. They would walk up to a player who would happily give them five or 10 minutes of his time. Now players kid they are on the telephone to avoid journalists or just refuse point blank to give interviews. In some ways it is the press's own fault. They've made it that way because it only needs one reporter to let a player down and that makes the whole team reluctant to trust the press in general.

If you are helpful to the press they tend to be kind to you in return. It applies in life generally that if a good guy is on the way up, he is usually given a smooth passage on the way down, whereas if someone is a sod on the way up, he will find life very difficult when things start going against him. Usually you'll reap what you sow.

Everybody has a job to do and I can't understand those players who refuse to co-operate with the media. Perhaps they should put themselves in the other man's court. If I was a journo trying to make a living I would want all the help sportsmen could give me. Football is big box office. It sells papers and TV coverage is reaching saturation levels. The players are paid unbelievable amounts but that doesn't excuse some of the bad publicity lads like Wayne Rooney have endured. They are only normal lads growing up, so they are going to do silly things like getting drunk from time to time. The last thing they want is someone standing in a corner of a bar somewhere with a camera waiting to catch them off guard.

When I was playing, the press in London hated us. It was just because we were winners that we were resented so much. The team at the top is always the most hated. I was reading the other day that Leeds United are still the most hated team in the country. Apparently it all dates back to our days under Don Revie, so we must have left a huge impression! There has certainly been nothing in recent years to make people hate the team.

Nowadays everyone who doesn't support Manchester United hates them because they are the outstanding team.

It's a burden that goes along with success. An unfortunate facet of the media in this country is that they build up stars and then delight in knocking them down. We don't read much about the lovely lad who has gone to the Olympics, won a medal, been the perfect son and lived the perfect life. They want to write something bad like the ban imposed on Christine Ohuruogu nine months before the British girl carried off the Olympic 400 metres gold medal. One national newspaper columnist slagged her off for missing drugs tests which led to the ban, later overturned. He wrote that as far as he was concerned, Ohuruogu hadn't won that medal. His piece was utter rubbish. As I said earlier, everybody makes mistakes—and hard drugs were certainly not involved. All sportsmen and women have to take tablets from time to time for various ailments. They can't be expected to know all the ingredients.

In the first chapter of this book John writes about his fall-out with Brian Clough, who spent just 44 days in charge of Leeds United after taking over from Don Revie. As an individual I never minded Clough despite some disparaging remarks he made at a dinner in Leeds when I was Yorkshire Television's 'Yorksport Personality of the Year'. I was always a self motivated individual so I didn't let Brian affect me, but he was a very difficult person to get on with. I never knew which side of the street I was on with him.

By the time he joined us he had lost the plot and his close companion, Peter Taylor, who could have settled him down and guided him a bit. Despite everything that happened in that short time at Leeds you had to admire his achievements at his other clubs. Telling us to throw in the bin the medals we had won under Don Revie was a bit heavy but it was just professional jealously because we had a good record against his club, Derby. Maybe it was also something to do with Brian and Don both coming from Middlesbrough. There was a bit of local rivalry and there is no doubt they hated each other.

My team-mates from the Revie era still get together from time to time for reunions and are always happy in each other's company. Many of us still watch the team and it's sad how far the club has fallen since the short time ago when we were in the Champions League.

I have no doubt that the freefall was down to bad management. You can't live dreams. You have to live reality and the reality is that we are now in League One because of some people's dreams. I just hope they can sleep at night without having nightmares. I feel confident that with Gary McAllister in charge, Leeds United are back on the right lines and I look forward to seeing us claw our way back to where we should be among the country's elite.

Peter Lorimer
October 2008

INTRODUCTION

SO YOU WANT TO BE A SPORTSWRITER?

It's a career most sports followers would cut off their right arm to pursue, but the life of a sportswriter isn't all glamour, as you'll discover in the following pages.

Rollickings from managers, coaches and players—hours spent waiting to interview sportsmen on draughty training grounds—long, laborious journeys to far flung venues—and laptops that insist on going slow with deadlines rapidly approaching. These are just some of the frustrations I've experienced during more than 40 years in journalism, mostly specialising in sport.

Yet when a job has enabled you to rub shoulders with boyhood heroes, taken you to some of Europe's best known sporting arenas and allowed you the privilege of travelling on the Leeds United team coach to FA Cup finals and a European Cup final, it would be churlish to complain.

From the late sixties onwards, I've known all the managers from Don Revie to Gary McAllister, players from Jack Charlton to Harry Kewell and his lower profile successors, and chairmen from Ald. Percy Woodward to Ken Bates.

This, though, is not solely a book about Leeds United (there have been enough of them to fill a library). Naturally, Elland Road and its inhabitants form the backcloth for most of my experiences. Yet, I've tried to make the book an entertaining insight into the life of a sportswriter in the hope that all those football fans who thought they were at a different match will understand just why.

From sub-editing a local football match between pub teams called Squinting Cat and Toby Jug to covering the 1975 European Cup final between Leeds United and Bayern Munich in Paris and much later interviewing that French enigma Eric Cantona—could there be starker contrasts in the duties of a sports journalist?

Leeds and Scotland goalkeeper David Harvey once told me he had long since learned the pen was mightier than the sword. I must admit that when struggling over whether to give a high or low mark to a player for his performance on the field I've tended to err on the generous side to those who have happily given me interviews.

Those with little or no time for the media have eventually got their 'comeuppance', as we say in Yorkshire. Sportsmen come and go, especially nowadays when loyal one-club men are almost unheard of, but sportswriters enjoy their jobs so much that they tend to hang around, just as I've done for those 40 years or so.

Despite covering top class football for a living, some of my happiest times were spent travelling with the Bramley Rugby League team when I worked for my first newspaper, the *Pudsey and Stanningley News*.

Every generation tends to believe its own era was the best and I've thanked my lucky stars countless times that I grew up in an era when characters abounded. England won the World Cup, Roger Bannister ran the first sub-four-minute mile, Fred Trueman and Brian Statham scared the living daylights out of Test batsmen, football pitches often resembled quagmires and Leeds and Chelsea could go at each other hammer and tongs without fear of finishing with three men a side!

I hope this book will appeal to football supporters, young journalists just starting out on their careers and seasoned reporters and sub-editors who can identify with many of my experiences. I hope, too, that those of you who have always regretted missing out on becoming a sportswriter won't change your mind after reading of the perils we hacks face.

Despite the job's frustrations, short of swinging a golf club or kicking a football, there are few better ways of earning a living if you truly love sport.

1

WHEN BRIAN CLOUGH WAS MR ANGRY

Shortly after 8.30am on my day off, the phone rang at home. On the line was one of football's most recognisable voices and the tone wasn't pleasant. 'Get your arse down here as quickly as you can, young man. We have things to discuss.'

There was no arguing with Brian Clough. Just days earlier, Leeds United chairman Manny Cussins had shocked football to the core by replacing England-bound Don Revie with Clough, Revie's arch enemy. If ever an appointment was doomed to failure this was it, but as a local newspaperman whose job was to cover Leeds United, I misguidedly looked on Clough's arrival as manna from heaven.

Was there ever a more controversial and newsworthy character than Clough? And here he was at Leeds United—the answer to a sportswriter's prayers. Yet that phone call and its immediate aftermath persuaded me that the man who had inspired Derby County to the League Championship and was later to take Nottingham Forest to two European Cup Final victories and a Super Cup triumph, had two sharply contrasting sides to his character.

I may have known little about him privately at the time but I did know that if you were summoned by BC—the initials emblazoned proudly on his tracksuit top—you turned up or took the consequences. At the last count I've had a working relationship with all 16 Leeds United managers, from Revie to Gary McAllister, and thoroughly enjoyed the company of most of them. Yet Clough's 44 days in charge during 1974 were sheer hell for many reasons.

It wasn't for lack of trying on my part, but BC never forgave me for writing a perfectly true story about unrest behind the scenes. There were strong rumours that Leeds' long-serving and much respected coach Syd Owen was considering leaving because he and others at the club couldn't get on with the new manager.

I quoted Syd who told me he did not intend to leave Leeds United 'at the moment', though I knew his old club Luton Town were ready to offer him a top post. Syd had also taken umbrage at Clough for overlooking him and sending trainer-coach Jimmy Gordon to Switzerland to spy on United's European Cup first round opponents FC Zurich. When I arrived at Clough's office, he was blazing. He always had a ruddy complexion and I feared he was about to explode. 'If we are going to get on, I can't have you writing stories like this,' he growled, stabbing a copy of my newspaper into my chest.

'But it's true, Brian, and I've toned it down,' I protested.

If I've learned anything from spending most of my working life with football people it is this: with very few exceptions they are right, you are wrong and if they think black is white you had better believe it. Once a footballer or manager gets it into his head that a reporter has stitched him up there is no persuading him otherwise—and you can be sure that before the day is out, the reporter's name will be mud with every member of the playing squad.

For that reason the local newspaperman treads a perilous tightrope. It's no use falling out with the players you need to interview on a regular basis. Yet Sports Editors demand stories that sell papers and readers quickly see through any reporter who thinks his or her job is to be an unofficial public relations officer for the club. I've been pinned against a dressing room wall by Dave Merrington when he was on the coaching staff at Elland Road, de-bagged by a bunch of boozed-up Bramley rugby league players on a bus passing through the centre of Oldham and blasted by manager Jimmy Adamson for turning up to catch the Leeds United team bus just five minutes early!

So, although I anticipated Clough's phone call, I never expected the words that followed my inevitable rollicking. 'Well, I've got that off my chest young man, now I expect you'll want a couple of exclusives!'

The sudden mood swing was remarkable by any standards. Having enjoyed an excellent relationship, for the most part, with Clough's predecessor Revie, I had no wish to fall out with BC, so just days before that telephone incident I agreed to take him on a house-hunting trip, reasoning that this would get us off on the right track. Whether he knew at that stage that his sojourn at Leeds would be as short-lived as 44 days I never found out, but when I turned up at Elland Road, Brian was watching his second favourite sport, cricket, on TV in the players' lounge. It was a Test match between England and Pakistan and, sprawling back in his armchair, Clough told me: 'Pour yourself a beer, young man, and we'll just watch a few overs.'

The time was 2.30pm. Several hours and many drinks later, my host decided the house-hunting trip was off for the day and I was in no condition to disagree. That meeting was friendly enough, but the offending Syd Owen story blew apart any semblance of a close working relationship with BC who thereafter insisted on referring to me as 'that ginger haired bastard from Bradford.'

He was wrong on two counts. Although I worked for Bradford's evening newspaper, the *Telegraph & Argus*, I was Leeds born and bred. As for being a bastard, my mother swears I was conceived on holiday at a Blackpool boarding house a full month after she and dad were married! Unfortunately, Brian Clough had an elephant's memory. Long after his departure from Elland Road, Leeds United played his team Nottingham Forest. As usual I joined the pack for the post-match press conference. To the surprise of the assembled hacks, Clough stopped answering one of their questions after spotting me and roared: 'Don't think you can stand there, young man. You did nothing for me when I was here at Leeds, so why should I do anything for you?'

In my view it was a totally unwarranted verbal attack and an embarrassing put-down. Some years later, at a similar press conference, BC actually apologised, telling me he had matured as a manager since our fall-out! My opinion of him changed somewhat after that—but not much. When Leeds sacked him, Clough received a reported tax-free golden handshake of £40,000 and was allowed to keep his club Mercedes. It was said that player power was responsible for his dismissal and there is no doubt that there was a huge personality clash between the manager and those highly experienced and successful players he had criticised so savagely in the past.

How would you feel if you were told to throw all your medals away because from now on you were going to win them honestly? Many players refused to sign new contracts after Clough's appointment and Leeds won only one league game out of six during BC's time at the helm, losing three and drawing two. They lost the FA Charity Shield to Liverpool on penalties, with Billy Bremner and Kevin Keegan sent off, and drew at Huddersfield in a League Cup tie—Clough's last game in charge. There was clearly no love lost between Clough and Manny Cussins. In fact, when I enquired after the chairman's health he quipped: 'I'm just going into hospital to have two Clough ulcers removed.'

I wasn't the only pressman to cross swords with BC, or Old Big Ed as he later dubbed himself after being awarded the OBE. At the press conference called by Leeds to mark his appointment, there were two amusing spats between the new manager and reporters. Colin Durkin, a ruddy faced and highly experienced court reporter, who also covered sport, was there for the Press Association. Colin began a question with the words, 'Mr Clough…'

Immediately the newly installed manager stopped him in his tracks. 'Hold on a minute, my friends call me Brian,' said BC, trying to set the right tone.

Undeterred, Colin, who was used to the formalities of the courtroom, proceeded, 'That's as maybe, Mr Clough, but we've only just met!'

For once Brian was left speechless and Colin continued with his question amid much mirth from his fellow hacks. Clough admonished Ronald Crowther, from the *Daily Mail*, for the tone of one of his questions, but Ron was no keener to back down than Colin had been. Sitting back in his chair with as much authority as he could summon, Ron looked BC in the eye and told him: 'I'll remind you Brian that it was the press who brought down Richard Nixon and he was a bigger man than you will ever be.'

That press conference must surely have persuaded Clough that he could expect a rough ride from the press corps during his time in West Yorkshire but he seemed determined to tough it out when he met Don Warters, from the Leeds-based *Yorkshire Evening Post*. Don had been away on holiday when BC arrived, so it was a week or so later when he turned up at Elland Road to introduce himself and ask a question about a story in that day's *Daily Mail*.

Bill Mallinson, the *Mail's* Yorkshire-based football writer at the time, had an exclusive story that five or six Leeds players were refusing to sign new contracts. Local reporter and new manager met in the club car park and once the pleasantries were out of the way, Don raised the subject of whether Bill's story was correct, so he could write a follow-up in that evening's paper. Clough was furious and told Don: 'You insult me by asking that question.'

As Don persisted, Clough's rage intensified and eventually

he blurted out: 'If you ask me that question again I'll kick you over that f***ing stand. Anyway there aren't five or six refusing to sign, there are nearer 10 or 12!'

After the chummy relationship so many of us had enjoyed with Revie, this was a totally new ball game and I have to admit that when those 44 days were over I breathed a huge sigh of relief. Having kicked the dust of Leeds off his feet, BC was appointed manager of Nottingham Forest in January, 1975, enjoying immense success as he turned arguably ordinary players into European Champions. He fell out with other journalists along the way but four men who formed a very close relationship with him were Gerald Mortimer, of the *Derby Evening Telegraph*, John Sadler, of *The Sun*, Vince Wilson, of the *Sunday Mirror*, and John Lawson, who wrote for the *Nottingham Evening Post* and later went freelance. All spoke very highly of Brian who treated them like sons and gave them countless stories. Good for them.

Despite the way he treated me and the Leeds players, I saw a very likeable side to BC. He loved his family with a passion and was never happier than when his 'bairns' were around him. Simon and Nigel, who were then aged just 10 and eight, respectively, were often seen happily kicking a football through the corridors of Elland Road. Nigel grew up to be an accomplished footballer and long-serving manager of Burton Albion.

So when I found myself covering a match between Farsley Celtic and Burton Albion in March, 2008, I had to pinch myself to believe almost 34 years had passed since I had last seen Nigel at Elland Road. I joined the throng of reporters interviewing him after Albion had beaten Farsley 1–0 in the Blue Square Premier League. I toyed with the idea of mentioning the link with his father, but decided against it. What was the point? He was probably sick of people constantly referring to him as Brian Clough's lad, anyway, so I let it pass.

When BC died, aged 69, on September 20, 2004, I preferred to remember his magnificent achievements with Derby and Forest rather than that bizarrely brief chapter of his career at Leeds which left football sages arguing for years whether he would have been successful eventually at Elland Road if Manny Cussins and most of his directors had shown more patience. We will never know the answer to that intriguing question.

One of my favourite Leeds players from that era was the legendary Billy Bremner, who later became the club's manager. Billy was as passionate about his football off the pitch as he was on it and his views were always forthright. He had played in an away game against Ipswich and picked up an injury. The rest of the players were travelling on to a game in Europe and at that stage the *Telegraph & Argus* didn't have the budget to send me along. So I shared a train carriage with Billy back to Leeds and we were busy debating the right of someone who had never played football professionally (me) to pass judgment in print on international players like Billy, Norman Hunter and Johnny Giles who were at the peak of their profession.

On the face of it, Billy's argument seemed sound and it was, and still is, shared by many sporting personalities. I attempted to convince Billy that my match reports were merely one man's opinion, to be agreed with or pilloried by my newspaper's readers as they saw fit. I wasn't setting myself up as an expert—just offering honest opinions.

Billy wasn't for backing down and he tried to enlist support for his argument from a fellow passenger whose face was familiar from my trips to the cinema. Richard Todd was the star of many a Hollywood blockbuster, including that war epic *The Dambusters*, and he had been taking an avid interest in our conversation.

It would have been easy for an actor very much in the public eye to side with a top footballer. After all, they were both in the entertainment industry. To my surprise, Richard replied that although he had sometimes suffered at the pen of critics, he valued their opinions if their views were constructive. Billy wasn't being nasty and I could sympathise with his viewpoint. After all, I wouldn't take kindly to someone who couldn't write or spell telling me how to do my job. You only have to listen to a group of football supporters arguing in the pub after a match to realise no two fans ever agree entirely. So what chance does a reporter have of avoiding accusations that he needs a white stick?

I had always admired Billy as a tenacious, multi-skilled footballer who repeatedly put his body on the line for the Leeds United cause—and I grew to respect him off the field too. Billy was a household name in the sixties and seventies when Leeds were in their prime and he was an inspiring captain of his club and Scotland. Yet he shunned the bright lights, for many years living in an unpretentious semi-detached house at Temple Newsam on the outskirts of Leeds.

When he moved to South Yorkshire he enjoyed nothing better than sharing a drink with miners from his village. How many of today's pampered super-stars actually mix with the supporters who pay their obscenely high wages? How many, too, give their home telephone number to trusted members of the press? It's hard enough to extract mobile numbers these days, yet I had every Leeds United player's home number in my contacts book. No-one from that era ever objected to being phoned at home, though I made it a rule never to ring at unsocial hours or pass on the numbers to other journalists.

In contrast, when I needed to make an urgent call to Gary Kelly, Leeds' Republic of Ireland international defender, who has since retired, he left me with a flea in my ear and made me feel like some stranger from a call centre. I had known Gary from the moment he arrived at the club as a junior and never let him down. Maybe I caught him at a bad moment, but at nearly twice his age I found it disrespectful to be treated in that way, especially as I had moved heaven and earth to interview all and sundry for his testimonial brochure.

To be fair to Gary, he often obliged me with interviews at the club's training ground and he donated the proceeds of his testimonial to charity after his sister had died of cancer. I also happen to know he made a substantial donation to the testimonial fund of former Leeds captain Lucas Radebe—an act of generosity that has never been made public until now.

There are far more demands on footballers from the media these days, of course, and I understand that. When I began covering Leeds United there were just two other reporters who regularly travelled to away matches on the team coach. Now there are so many radio stations, websites and print publications that the days when reporters travelled with top teams have long gone.

Those trips were the highlight of the week for me— rubbing shoulders with the cream of British footballers, enjoying their banter and joining in their card schools. I was put on trust, knowing that anything I overheard was off the record or I would be kicked off the bus in future. Managers and players took me into their confidence because they knew I wouldn't let them down.

It was possible to pick up the phone and chat to legendary Liverpool manager Bill Shankly at Anfield on his private line, providing it was between 9.30am and the start of training— and on occasions the great man would even answer the switchboard phone if he was passing. How times change.

Relationships between Sir Alex Ferguson and the press hit such a low ebb at one stage that the Manchester United supremo would allow just one journalist from the written national media to interview him the day before a match, on the understanding that the quotes were passed on to the rest of the pack. John Bond, the former Manchester City manager, was so publicity conscious that he held a briefing session with the press about an hour before every home match when he was in charge at Norwich, explaining the formation of his team, the reason for any changes in personnel and the tactics to be adopted. I found Joe Royle, Ron Atkinson and many more big name managers similarly amiable.

Yet it wasn't all glamour, as I quickly discovered in my first journalistic job on the quaintly named *Pudsey and Stanningley News*.

2

TOBY JUG VERSUS SQUINTING CAT

Eric Gooseman was a newspaper Editor who, it seemed to me, carried the problems of the world on his shoulders. After giving me my first job in journalism, maybe he had! Goosie, as he was affectionately known to employees of the *Pudsey and Stanningley News*, seemed to possess a permanent mouth ulcer which caused him acute discomfort. I assumed that was the cause of the old man's furrowed brow and not my verbatim reports from Pudsey Town Council and the local magistrates' court. These were two of many proceedings I had to cover in addition to my beloved sports reporting.

Goosie had retired from the *Scarborough Evening News* and his main claims to fame were selling his house to England fast bowler 'Fiery' Fred Trueman and spending a year as president of the Editors' Guild. He was intensely proud of both. The duties of a local weekly newspaper Editor were, in theory, less arduous than overseeing several editions of an evening publication every day. Yet the downside for Goosie was taking charge of a small, inexperienced staff of reporters who were learning their trade and inevitably making cock-ups along the way.

The *Pudsey and Stanningley News* was owned by the Harrogate-based Ackrill Group and colleagues told me at the time that the policy seemed to be to sack anyone who completed his or her indentures (apprenticeship) so they wouldn't qualify for senior rates of pay! They found any excuse, I was told, to administer the order of the boot. Reporter Revel Barker, informed that his work at the *Pudsey and Stanningley News* was sub-standard, was immediately hired by the *Daily Mirror* where he spent many happy and successful years.

Lots of others made the grade on evening and national papers—testimony to the thorough training provided at the *Pudsey and Stanningley News*. In those days people paid for weeklies and they had big circulations. There was a real sense of community and readers were intensely loyal—until a reporter had the audacity to criticise members of the amateur dramatic society for their abysmal efforts and fluffed lines. Damning reports usually produced angry letters to the Editor who, to his credit, always backed his staff against 'those poofter prima donnas'. Mind you, there was no shortage of thespian talent in the area. Intake High School, in Bramley, had such a high reputation for drama that it recruited countless pupils for parts in *Coronation Street* and other TV programmes.

Perhaps the most renowned ex Intake pupil to appear in *Coronation Street* is Jack P. Shepherd, who has played that insidious rascal David Platt for many years. Considering that *Coronation Street* is supposed to be set in the heart of Lancashire, I've always found it amusing that many of the cast have broad Yorkshire accents. Spice girl Mel B is an ex Intake pupil, too, and the late Jake Thackray, who found fame on TV and on record in the sixties and seventies with his quirky songs, was an English teacher at the school.

No news story or football match was too insignificant for *Pudsey and Stanningley News* coverage and I well remember sub-editing a match report between pub teams called Toby Jug and Squinting Cat. I can't remember the score but spilt milk inevitably appeared somewhere in the headline! From Toby Jug versus Squinting Cat to covering the European Cup

Final between Bayern Munich and Leeds United at the magnificent Parc des Princes Stadium in Paris, or interviewing that prince of French footballers Eric Cantona—could there be a sharper contrast in anyone's journalistic duties?

To give you some idea of how small-time the *Pudsey and Stanningley News* was, my first job title on leaving Allerton Grange School in Leeds was Sports Editor. That description conjures up visions of a highly qualified sports journalist with a busy team of reporters and sub-editors under his command. Not so at the *Pudsey and Stanningley News*. I was a sporting one-man band, thrown in at the deep end and told to get on with it because, apart from his Fred Trueman connection, Goosie washed his hands of sport completely and the budget didn't run to two members of the sports staff. My predecessor had already left, so I had to learn the rudiments of typography and page lay-out as I went along. Some of my early efforts at page design make me wince when I recall them, but they say you learn by your mistakes. As a sports fanatic in my schooldays I was an avid reader of sports reports in the local and national press, so I had some idea about how to construct a report. Strangely, though, for someone who lived for rugby, football and cross-country running at school, and who always gained top marks in English and bottom marks in maths and technical drawing, becoming a sports journalist had never occurred to me. If you stayed on to do your GCE A-levels, the teaching staff assumed you would go to teacher-training college or university. That option never appealed to me because I wanted to quit the classroom and get out there to earn some cash.

Although I didn't realise it at the time, the seeds of a journalistic career were sown while I was at junior school in the fifties. Every year, Leeds schools ran a trip to the Rugby League Cup final at Wembley—a day out that hundreds of kids eagerly anticipated. We made the journey by rail and our parents made sure we were up extra early to catch the train to King's Cross from Leeds Central Station, which sadly is no more.

This was in the days of steam and, as most of us were train-spotters, the journey to London was spent scribbling numbers into notebooks that became grubbier as the miles went by. Many of the locomotives we saw carried names and the spellings I learned in those far off days have helped me countless times in my adult life. The Rugby League Cup final was the day's highlight, of course, and on the return journey we all had an essay to write on our impressions of the trip. There was a prize for the best essay in each carriage of the train, with the winners' names appearing in the evening paper. I had the good fortune to have my essay chosen, so my name appeared in print for the first time—and was I proud!

My grandparents lived in Blackpool so, during the school holidays, I stayed with them and enjoyed watching the Blackpool Borough Rugby League team when they played at the old St Anne's Road greyhound stadium. The site is now a housing estate but I have vivid memories of being a ball boy before the bulldozers moved in and Blackpool Borough moved to Borough Park in the centre of the town. My claim to 'fame' at the time was to catch a ball that had been kicked high into the sky by a Blackpool player whose name escapes me and return it to a St Helens legend. I well remember the name of the player who took the ball from me after my spectacular catch—South African winger Tom Van Vollenhoven—one of the most famous Rugby League players of his day. I dreamed about that moment for weeks afterwards.

I was an avid supporter of the Leeds Rugby League club, too, and my favourite player was the gifted Welshman Lewis Jones who kicked the ball prodigious distances and was equally effective as a stand-off or centre. It always amused me when my elders told me Leeds relied on Lewis Jones and Leeds United relied on Jewish loans.

With a career in sports journalism a long way from my thoughts, my careers master at school considered the police force would suit me—presumably because I had always been a 'plodder'. I was seriously considering that avenue when a friend of my parents spotted an advert in the *Pudsey and Stanningley News*. It read: 'Junior reporter wanted, keen on sport. Apply to Mr E. Gooseman, Editor, stating qualifications.'

Although I was born in 1946—the baby boom year after the Second World War—there were lots of jobs, so school-leavers could more or less pick and choose. Not like today when even university-educated candidates find themselves up against 100 or more rivals for the same post and sometimes end up stacking shelves at Morrisons. I duly wrote off for an interview, was granted an audience with Mr Gooseman and, as I mentioned earlier, landed the job of Sports Editor. At the same time I was a general news reporter and performed every duty from making the tea to gathering the names of mourners at funerals, on a starting wage, I think, of £7 per week.

I spent five years at the *Pudsey and Stanningley News*, receiving a thorough education in all aspects of journalism and life, which was never dull. One of the favourite pastimes of the printers was to reduce the rodent population by hurling slugs of type at the offending creatures. Naturally, the more squeamish members of the reporting staff stayed well clear of the printing works when culls were in full flow. After one memorable lunchtime escapade, the paper's photographer and entire reporting staff came close to being sacked and reported to the police.

Photographer Peter Taglione, a heavyweight Tommy Cooper look-alike, had an artistic bent—he greatly admired the female form, hence his membership of a camera club where models were encouraged to take up erotic poses for the lens. No problem there, except Peter fancied his chances of persuading a member of the paper's reporting staff to have her picture taken, scantily clad, in a copse of trees on a local farm that lunchtime. No sooner had the brazen hussy agreed, than the news spread through the office faster than a Peter Lorimer shot at goal. Taglione and his 'model' made their way to the farm, not realising the rest of us were following at what we took to be a safe distance.

The reporter had just undressed and taken up her first pose when the booming voice of the farmer could be heard bellowing at the pair to scarper or he would fetch the police. The farmer had spotted the rest of us too and, unfortunately, Peter's van had the name and phone number of our newspaper boldly emblazoned on its side. By the time we returned to the office, Goosie had received a graphic account of our scurrilous behaviour and left us in no doubt that any repeat would result in the sack.

Taglione was one of those naturally funny characters. You only had to look at him to burst into fits of laughter. When the even more hilarious Tommy Cooper was appearing at Batley Variety Club and agreed to knock over a pile of pennies at The Rock public house in Bramley, a few miles from the *Pudsey and Stanningley News* office, Peter went along to take the picture. The memory of two 'Tommy Coopers' in the same room cracking jokes has remained with me to this day. Sadly, both have passed on, but what fun they must be having in Heaven!

Then there was the time the *Monty Python's Flying Circus* team visited Pudsey to film a sketch for the hugely popular TV series. Some genius had decided to make Pudsey's tiny railway station the centre of the universe in an hilarious plot involving John Cleese *et al*. Although the sketch was quite short when it appeared on TV, filming took all day and provided this reporter with an excuse to leave the office for hours on end, mixing with the stars.

The actors' capers on the platform, as trains hurtled through the station, left disbelieving passengers doing a double-take, suspecting they were dreaming. For me, at that time, Pudsey probably was the centre of the universe as I relished my formative years learning the newspaper journalist's trade. Although the *Pudsey and Stanningley News* had its own office and printing works, the paper's owners, Ackrills, had a much more modern plant in Harrogate, so every Wednesday the pages, in metal form, were loaded into a van and driven from Pudsey to Harrogate to be printed.

The once-a-week trip afforded me the chance to play an enjoyable game of five-a-side football with the lads from the Harrogate office as we waited for the page proofs to appear for checking. One Wednesday our game was cut short amid a full scale emergency. Two or three pages were dropped as they were being transported from the van into the printing works. Countless slugs of type were 'pied', as the printers called it when lines of type were accidentally jumbled up, and it took so long to put those pages back together that, for the first time in living memory, the *Pudsey and Stanningley News* was in danger of missing the newsagents' stands on Thursday morning.

Fortunately, everyone rallied round, the printers were on double time and burning the midnight oil paid off, though I don't recall receiving a penny extra for all those hours hanging around, waiting for the page proofs to appear. Somehow the bosses regarded journalism as a vocation, while the printers, strengthened by powerful unions, drove a hard bargain and carried off much heavier pay packets. New technology was to change all that, of course, as Eddie Shah and others like him held sway and the golden era of the print worker passed into history.

The *Pudsey and Stanningley News* office, in the town centre, was once adorned by photos galore of events captured by Peter Taglione's ubiquitous lens. Prints of weddings and sporting teams, in particular, sold like hot cakes in a town where everyone seemed to know everyone else and that office was a focal point for the community. Sadly, it closed many years ago and the building is now home to a pet shop, a fast food outlet and a hairdresser's.

3

RIGHT SCORE, WRONG SCORERS

Pudsey, of course, apart from being the birthplace of *Children In Need*'s Pudsey Bear, spawned such cricketing legends as Sir Leonard Hutton and Ray Illingworth, so the local inhabitants take their cricket very seriously.

Pudsey St Lawrence and Farsley were the two major Bradford League clubs from our circulation area and, as well as covering their affairs for the *Pudsey and Stanningley News*, I earned a few quid by telephoning reports and scores to two Saturday sports papers. These were the green edition of the *Yorkshire Evening Post*, published in Leeds, and the pink *Yorkshire Sports*, published in Bradford by the *Telegraph & Argus*. At the end of the game I also had to phone in the score to Crabtree's Agency, which compiled the league's results and sent them round the Sunday papers. It was my introduction to freelance journalism—a route I was to follow full time much later in my career.

Fortunately, the fixtures were arranged so that games involving Pudsey St Lawrence and Farsley didn't clash, so there was a weekly bonus in income for this impoverished reporter. Unfortunately it was the pre-mobile era and although the comparatively posh St Lawrence had a phone in their Tofts Road clubhouse, the nearest public phone to Farsley's Red Lane ground was in a call box half a mile down a steep hill in the village.

The order for the pink involved filing 150 words after a few overs, followed by a further 75 words and details of the score to date. If that call box was working, having escaped Farsley's young vandals, you were lucky, and if it was vacant that was a real bonus. Getting copy into the newspaper offices on time was essential, yet so often I was left cursing as some love-struck teenager insisted on babbling down the phone to her boyfriend, without a moment's thought for the lengthening queue outside. It was at such times that a return to pigeon post seemed almost appealing and eventually, after several blasts from sports desk staff for late copy, I struck up an arrangement with a local resident to use his home phone instead.

Those reports never amounted to much because, for deadline reasons, they covered only the matches' early stages. The opening bowlers and early order batsmen were usually the only players to get a mention, so the same names would crop up week after week and headlines tended to be on the lines of 'Farsley make steady start' or 'Pudsey's quick breakthrough'. I am convinced sub-editors had a stock of pre-written headlines to suit most states of play, yet despite the mundane reading matter, copies of the pink, especially, sold like hot cakes after being rushed to Bradford League grounds.

Farsley Celtic were, and still are, the main football team in the Pudsey area and I remember having to stand on the touchline in all weathers at the quaintly named Throstle Nest, taking notes for the *Pudsey and Stanningley News*. I was lucky to get a team sheet before the game and even luckier if it contained up-to-date changes. Before getting to know the Farsley players by sight I obtained a team sheet and, not realising there had been late changes, I got the identities of half the team wrong, including three of the four scorers! Players, officials and spectators read the *Pudsey and Stanningley News* avidly and my embarrassment was only matched by Goosie's rage when the complaints poured in.

If that incident had happened on completion of my indentures I'd have been out of a job for sure but, presumably because I was cheap, I survived to visit Throstle Nest many more times, making sure any late team changes were duly noted. The club's rapid rise through the leagues took them into the Blue Square Premier—just one leap away from the Football League—and happily I have found myself covering the club again when Leeds United are away from home, though the Celts were relegated after just one season in the Blue Square Premier.

Throstle Nest is one of those homespun, friendly grounds whose facilities haven't quite kept pace with the club's progress on the pitch. There is a press area of sorts—a working bench which, until well into the 2007–08 season, was barely large enough for four journalists to work in comfort. In practice, local and visiting radio men and their equipment took half the seats, leaving most writers in the overflow seats with no writing bench.

The bench doubled in length towards the end of the season but unbelievably in these days of modern communications there was still no electrical point for laptops in the press area. Those needing to plug in a laptop required a long extension lead stretching from what passes for the directors' box. And they had to arrive at the ground very early or they would find the extension lead already claimed by someone else. I've raised the power-point issue several times with club officials, so far without any positive result, but one day...

At least I got the score right at the end of that never to be forgotten experience at Farsley when I got most of the scorers wrong. Others have not been so fortunate and I remember a well respected reporter called Noel Wilde filing through an incorrect score to the *Sunday Mirror* from a major match involving Leeds United. The referee disallowed a late goal but Noel was so busy dictating his report to a copytaker that he was the only person on the ground not to notice the disallowed goal. Naturally, merciless fellow journalists teased and tormented him about it for weeks, though it was a case of 'there but for the grace of God go I.'

Ian Dennis, who now works for Radio Five Live, was employed by BBC Radio Leeds when Leeds United played Spartak Moscow at Elland Road in a UEFA Cup match, in December, 1999. Leeds won 1–0, making the aggregate from the two legs of the tie 2–2. Ian thought there would be extra time and was busily building up the tension when he noticed Leeds players were celebrating on the pitch. The alarm bells started to ring before Ian and his summariser Norman Hunter finally realised Leeds had won the tie on the away goal rule. Ian is one of the BBC's most respected and gifted radio commentators, but he still has nightmares about that UEFA Cup blunder.

I spent much of my time at the 'Newsy Puds' covering the Bramley Rugby League team. Having been born in the village of Bramley, Leeds, and attended junior school there, covering the local team was the proverbial dream come true. Bramley, known as the Villagers, were the friendliest and most down to earth club imaginable. Apart from their finest hour—winning the BBC Floodlit Trophy—they had never threatened the dominance enjoyed by the likes of Leeds, Wigan or St Helens. My interest in the Villagers began when our school received a batch of free tickets and I caught the Rugby League bug.

Those football clubs who price out youngsters should take a leaf out of Bramley's book by using a free ticket sprat to catch the mackerels who are the paying customers of the future. Bramley's generosity certainly paid off as I paid to pass through their turnstiles many times before becoming a ball boy and later covering their matches for the local paper.

In those days, players didn't arrive at the ground by car.

They shared a bus ride with supporters and drank with the fans. Bramley's original ground, the Barley Mow, was conveniently situated behind a pub of the same name and as the players left the field some of them had a refreshing pint of bitter waiting for them before they headed off to the baths! In fact I can testify that the Bramley players of the time lived mainly on a diet of beer—a far cry from the super-fit Rugby League players of today. One of my favourites, both as a player and a man, was long-serving prop forward Dave Horn, who worked as a drayman for Tetley's brewery in Leeds.

Dave, built like a tank, wore the Bramley shirt through three decades and usually scored his tries with two or three opponents hanging round his neck. He typified many of the characters Bramley produced over the years. Hard as they come, he never gave less than maximum effort despite many a quarrel with the club's directors in his role as players' spokesman. Dave would often invite me, along with his team-mates, back to his home in Pudsey where we would sink what seemed the equivalent of a barrel between us. On one memorable occasion we enjoyed Dave's usual hospitality and left in typically legless fashion. The next day Bramley dished out a thrashing to Dewsbury in a Challenge Cup tie. So much for match preparation!

Mention of Dave Horn reminds me of a Player of the Season competition run by the cigarette brand Players No 6. There was a prize for the guy judged Player of the Match by the press and a separate award for the player voted for by spectators. Voting forms were distributed among the crowd and naturally the player with the most votes was named Player of the Match. The votes also counted towards a Player of the Season award and a table of the leading contenders was regularly issued during the campaign.

Now Dave was a good forward at this level, but Rugby League fans outside Bramley, of which there were many, couldn't understand why his name consistently figured at, or near, the top of the voting table. Maybe they should have visited the Bramley dressing room and stands on match-days to see Dave and his pals filling in forms galore in favour of the popular prop forward!

Another Bramley stalwart remembered with special affection was Jim Hainsworth, a giant prop who always had a dew-drop suspended from his nose. It remained a source of wonderment to me that, once play had started, the globule never left its precarious perch until the final whistle sounded.

During my spell as a ball-boy, Bramley paid me the princely sum of six old pence and I earned every penny. The Villagers had a Maori full back, Johnny Wilson, whose prodigious goal-kicking brought mixed blessings. The lad who stood in awe, watching his hero kicking goals from all angles and distances, spent much of his time retrieving the ball from Bramley Town Street. Such was Wilson's power that he regularly kicked the ball out of the ground, causing me to run off in pursuit.

During my time covering Bramley, home and away, I suffered the humiliation of a de-bagging. Dave Horn and some of his pals reckoned I'd been a bit harsh on them in a report of their latest match so, on the way back from a game in Lancashire, they took their revenge. The team bus was passing through the centre of Oldham when I was set upon by a posse of players who had my trousers round my ankles quicker than it takes to whisk a ball into the scrum. Fortunately, my embarrassment was limited because there were so few pedestrians on the streets at the time, but those who witnessed the scene must have thought they were watching the making of a gay porn film!

Bramley's days as a professional club were numbered as fewer spectators passed through the turnstiles. Eventually McLaren Field, which had replaced the Barley Mow ground, was sold off for housing development, even though the will of Mrs Edith McLaren had decreed it should be used solely for sporting purposes. They've named the housing estate after

Mrs McLaren but she must still be turning in her grave at the flagrant disregard for her last wishes.

I nearly dug my own grave when I was placed in charge of the *Pudsey and Stanningley News* during one of the Editor's holidays. That weekend the *News of the World* (or *News of the Screws*, as we called it) featured a Bramley couple who, it claimed, had been offering sexual favours at their home. Naturally it was the talk of the district and, as the Bramley area was on my patch, I weighed in with a front page story.

The couple had fled by the time I knocked on their door on the Monday morning after the story had broken in the *News of the World*, but neighbours spoke of the many comings and goings there had been at the house. When he read the proof of my story, the Managing Editor of our newspaper group hit the roof. How did I know the *News of the Screws'* allegations were correct, he rightly demanded to know, and was it my intention to have our paper sued? A replacement front page story was hurriedly found before my inexperience could risk the *Pudsey and Stanningley News* receiving a libel claim.

4

FRED TRUEMAN ON THE WARPATH

After completing my training at the age of 23 at the _Pudsey and Stanningley News_, which included deputising for the Editor when Goosie was on holiday or had a day off, it was time to move on. Edgar Craven, a charming man much liked by the _Pudsey and Stanningley News_ staff, had taken over from the retired Goosie but he, too, was drawing his pension and when he left I was offered the Editorship.

I turned it down for two reasons. Firstly, and most importantly, I felt I needed to gain more experience, possibly on an evening newspaper, before deigning to fill an Editor's chair. Secondly, the money offered for the job fell £2 a week below the offer I had received to join the _Telegraph & Argus_ as a general reporter with opportunities to cover sport!

To this day I don't know whether I made the right decision, though the _Telegraph & Argus_ brought me immense enjoyment, travel to Europe and beyond with Leeds United and the opportunity to mix with some of football's biggest names. We can all look back on one decision in our lives and mark it out as a defining moment. Opting to reject the Editor's chair was mine. Not that I waved news gathering goodbye. While on the news staff of the _Telegraph & Argus_, I interviewed Margaret Thatcher when she was Education Secretary before she took over at Number 10, and I found her far more charming than the Iron Lady she was to become. I also covered rare visits to the area by Edward Heath, Prince Charles and Cliff Richard and once fell out with Fred Trueman for turning up on his doorstep near the Dales village of Gargrave.

I was there to investigate stories that Fred was seeing a local lady who later became his wife. Fortunately, as it turned out, 'Fiery Fred' wasn't there, but the future Mrs Trueman was and, of course, she later informed Fred of the uninvited visit from a *Telegraph & Argus* reporter and photographer. Soon after returning to the office I took a call from a furious F.S. Trueman who, as many a batsman will testify, was a fearsome character when riled. The language was choice by any standards. Suffice to say Fred threatened to leave me unable to father a child if I ever showed up in Gargrave again. It is a village I studiously avoided until Fred's death in 2006.

A similar character to F.S. Trueman is show-jumping legend Harvey Smith, another proud Yorkshireman who calls a spade a 'bloody shovel' and has crossed swords with his sport's hierarchy on many occasions. Harvey's stables are at High Eldwick, near Bingley, in the *Telegraph & Argus's* circulation area, so it was inevitable that, sooner or later, I would be sent to interview him. My meeting with Harvey came just days after he made international headlines by raising a V-sign towards Douglas Bunn, show director of the Wills British Jumping Derby, at Hickstead. Harvey won the event but was disqualified by Bunn for 'making a disgusting gesture towards the show's directors.'

Harvey was in no mood for apologies as he told me: 'I won and there is nothing anyone can do about that. I made the V-sign because I won the event. You do silly things when you win, because you are so tensed up during the actual ride. You need half an hour to unwind afterwards. The whole thing is a personal vendetta between Mr Bunn and me. Mr Bunn's own rules do not override the international ones. He has to sign the [£2,000] cheque.'

Whether Harvey won that particular battle I can't recall, but there were many more arguments to come between the great man and show-jumping's establishment. Good for him. Sport needs characters like Harvey Smith—especially those sports that would normally struggle to justify a paragraph near the foot of a column to raise their profile.

When I joined the *Telegraph & Argus* it was a campaigning broadsheet newspaper under the dynamic editorship of Peter Harland, who later went to the Sunday Times. Deputy News Editor was Raymond Fitzwalter, a sharp-witted young man who had been the first to expose John Poulson, the corrupt architect, who shot to national infamy in what became known as The Poulson Affair. Granada Television snapped up Ray as an investigative reporter who became editor of *World in Action*, the programme that exposed crooked individuals and regimes. The *Telegraph & Argus's* news editor was a wily old fox called Harry Williams who, it seemed to me at the time, must have been in his eighties. In fact, he was much younger and had a laid back style which belied his keen grasp of a good story and how to get it.

Harry also had a warped sense of humour. For instance, he would look around the office and ask: 'Were any of you in the Boy Scouts?' Someone would respond positively, whereupon Harry would look him in the eye and declare, 'Oh good, you're just the man to cover a jumble sale in Keighley.'

There was no connection whatsoever between the Boy Scouts and the jumble sale, of course, but Harry had his 'volunteer' for the most mundane job on that day's diary. Shortly before Helen and I were married in 1971 she came into the *Telegraph & Argus* office wearing a mini-skirt, knee-length white boots and a head-band. She looked fabulous and Harry looked her up and down, gave me a knowing look and whispered: 'Very nice lad, but can she cook Yorkshire puddings?' Unfortunately the answer was—and still is—no!

Editor Harland certainly knew how to motivate his staff.

Exclusive stories were rewarded not only with large by-lines, but usually an extra tenner in the weekly wage packet and a hand-written thank you note. It was hard to know which note was more gratefully received, though on reflection it was probably the tenner!

It was sports-minded Harland who wisely decided that because Leeds United were so successful and Elland Road was little more than 10 miles from the *Telegraph & Argus* office, the paper should have a specialist reporter covering the club. Don Warters was given the job and I had to bide my time.

My first day at the *Telegraph & Argus* left me completely knackered. It was supposed to be a gentle 8.30am to 4pm shift during which I would familiarise myself with the building and my new colleagues. Instead I was to write a front page story about a tragic event that made national television news and kept me on duty for nearly 24 hours.

A police inspector and night-watchman had been gunned down at a Farsley mill and a massive hunt was launched to catch the killer. Police killings have always created immense public interest and Farsley suddenly became a magnet for the national and international media. I was sent to cover the story because of my local connections and I duly filed about 30 paragraphs of atmospheric copy and quotes gathered from a stint of door-knocking. I still have a copy of that night's *Telegraph & Argus*. The headline read: 'Doors locked in village of fear'—by John Wray.

Looking back, I was hooked on the ego trip every journalist enjoys from seeing his or her name on the front page or anywhere else in the paper for that matter. For the record, the killer was apprehended, found guilty and given a life sentence.

Another story which attracted national interest landed in my lap when I happened to phone the normally meticulous speaking clock and found it was 10 minutes late! The fault lasted for 20 minutes and I was amused by a spokesman's attempt to explain away the mistake. The voice on the speaking clock had sounded perfectly clear to me, but the spokesman told me distortion on the line was to blame for the error. The correct time had been relayed from equipment in Liverpool and London, he claimed.

Because of my background as Sports Editor of the *Pudsey and Stanningley News*, I was allowed to cover Rugby League and occasional Huddersfield Town football matches for the *Telegraph & Argus* while still employed on the news staff. However, my lucky break came when Don Warters, who, as I mentioned earlier, had been the paper's Leeds United reporter, left to join the Leeds-based *Yorkshire Evening Post*. During part of my time at the *Pudsey and Stanningley News*, I compiled a Leeds United form report on each player because Don Revie's team had emerged as one of the top sides in the country, attracting immense interest. As well as providing a different angle on United's matches, it gave me an excuse to gain entry to the joys of Elland Road's press box when I wasn't covering the Bramley Rugby League team.

Football reporters for the nationals were so well known in those days that placards bearing their names were plastered on fences or lampposts leading to the ground. The *Daily Express* placard, for instance, would proudly proclaim: 'Desmond Hackett is here today', while the *Mirror* would boast 'Read Frank McGhee, only in the *Mirror*'. Such names were like today's pop stars to a young journalist on the first rungs of the career ladder and to mix with them was every bit as exciting. So when the vacancy for a Leeds United reporter came up at the *Telegraph & Argus*, I was first to volunteer my services. To begin with, I remained on the *Telegraph & Argus*'s news staff but also covered Leeds United stories and matches. The mix was never going to work because United would call a press conference while I was out covering a murder or a bus strike.

After one particularly harrowing experience, my request to move into the sports department full time was granted and I've been a specialist sports writer ever since. The event that persuaded me to quit news coverage happened during an otherwise quiet day in the newsroom. Then, at about 2pm, the News Editor at the time, Don Alred, whose police contacts were second to none, told me to visit a recently bereaved family. I was to find out as much as I could about the victim and try to borrow a photograph for the next day's paper.

Nothing unusual about that, I thought. No journalist enjoys the task of interviewing a family recently bereaved. Yet in this case I unwittingly found myself breaking news of the death to the victim's brother and sister **before** their parents or the police had told them. A teenage lad had been found dead at the foot of an electricity pylon and investigations were at a very early stage. Unaware that the kids were alone in the house I knocked on the door, announced that I was from the *Telegraph & Argus* and foolishly asked if I could speak to the parents of the dead lad.

The kids immediately and not surprisingly burst into tears. Their parents had gone to the scene of the discovery to identify the body and, after I made sure a neighbour was looking after the distraught youngsters, I set off for the office, only to meet the parents returning home in a police car. I fully understood their rage on discovering that a reporter had broken the news to their children and I knew no amount of apologies would console them. It wasn't my colleague Don Alred's fault that the police had released the boy's name and address to the *Telegraph & Argus*, but I felt sick to the pit of my stomach for days afterwards.

Don was an amiable, portly pipe-smoking character who, as well as his news editing duties, covered Bradford City football club for the paper. As enthusiastic in his sixties as he had been as a fresh-faced cub reporter, Don would eagerly wait for each day's first edition of the *Telegraph & Argus* to arrive on his desk and bawl across at the sub-editors: 'Where's my by-line, kid?' Don expected his name to appear on every piece he wrote and if a sub-editor omitted his by-line, the 'offender' soon knew about it!

Don's approach to covering his beloved Bradford City contrasted sharply with my methods when I became the paper's Leeds United reporter. Before submitting his copy to the sub-editors, Don would often phone Bradford City's manager and dictate his report for approval. I would never have dreamed of seeking Don Revie's blessing for my stories. After all, it would have been a form of censorship and I am sure Revie had more important priorities than going through my reports with a fine tooth comb. When I queried Don Alred's approach, his explanation was: 'When you've been covering a club as long as I have, kid, you'll learn that you get more stories by staying on the right side of your contacts.'

That was true, of course, but I haven't changed my opinion that Don's relationship with those in charge at Bradford City was too close to allow him sufficient impartiality. I remember an occasion when Bradford City lost heavily, while the local Rugby League club, Bradford Northern (now known as Bradford Bulls), won by a margin of about 80 points. Don's match report about the luckless Bantams was in sharp contrast to Brian Smith's critical verdict on Northern who, he felt, should have beaten a weak Blackpool Borough side by 100 points or more!

At no time have I had my opinions in a match report changed by a sub-editor and I am indebted to all of them for that. However, I do know of one evening newspaper Editor, no less, who took a dislike to his local team's top goal-scorer because the player had been rude to him at a function they attended. From then on, the Editor insisted on his reporter giving the player low marks for performance. I'm not sure I could have tolerated interference of that kind for long before handing in my notice or seeking other duties.

Many local reporters tend to be biased in favour of the team they cover, but readers see through praise without occasional criticism like a plate of glass. Some reporters get round the 'problem' by praising the opposition when their own team has under-performed, but you can only take that course so many times before being rumbled.

Thankfully I have never again gone through anything as traumatic as that experience with the bereaved family, though my sports-writing career hasn't been without its dramas, by any means.

5

BAD TIMING
AND THE TEAM BUS

My first two matches covering Leeds United for the *Telegraph & Argus* could hardly have been more contrasting. The first was a pre-season friendly at Doncaster's ramshackle Belle Vue ground. The second was an unrivalled Match of the Day at Manchester United's theatre of dreams.

Doncaster were beaten 2–1, Mick Jones scoring early on before Leeds' Welsh international goalkeeper Gary Sprake suffered one of his infamous lapses in concentration to let in a 30 yard equaliser from former Leeds forward Rod Johnson. Jack Charlton headed the winner against Doncaster and another header—this time from Mick Jones—saw Revie's side win a close contest at Old Trafford.

Before that Doncaster game I clearly remember reporting for my first of many journeys on the team bus. Don Revie and his players had dined at the Queens Hotel in Leeds city centre before the short trip and I had arranged to meet up with them after the meal. I arrived a little late but was just in time to hail the team bus as it made its way round the roundabout in City Square. Don stopped the bus to let me on as the players struck up a predictable chorus of 'Fares please'. Most footballers may have left school at 15 but their wit is razor sharp, especially when it's at the expense of the press. Nor did I escape a telling-off from Revie for being late and arriving without a shirt and tie. I thought I looked smart in polo-neck sweater and jacket, but Don left me in no doubt that my dress sense needed to improve if I was to travel with the team in future.

Many years later, when Jimmy Adamson was manager, United had a European tie against Valletta, in Malta, and the press were told to catch the team bus outside the hotel at 1.30pm. At 1.20pm precisely, a couple of us left our rooms and made our way to the coach. There wasn't a soul in sight so we went back to our rooms, returning five minutes later to be greeted by a nearly full bus and a furious Adamson tapping his watch. I'll never forget his words.

'What time do you fellas call this?' he demanded to know in his heavy north-east accent.

'But we're still five minutes early, Jim,' I protested.

Back came the unbelievable retort: 'If you were catching a plane would you turn up at the airport five minutes before take-off?'

There was no arguing with Adamson who was anxious to get on his way to the stadium. We sheepishly took our places on the coach as the players struggled unsuccessfully to control their laughter.

On our trips abroad it never ceased to amaze me that, with a few exceptions, the players had no interest in sightseeing. Even when they had free time, for the most part, they would stay in their hotel which could have been anywhere in the world. They did not consider Rome's magnificent historical buildings, the Kremlin in Moscow and Milan's exclusive shops worthy of a glance.

I was amazed to find a TGI Friday's restaurant less than 200 metres from our hotel in the centre of Moscow in an underground shopping complex. The menu was identical to the one at home but the prices were roughly halved. A few months later I was watching the news on TV and a bomb had gone off in that same complex!

The Wray family have a spooky habit of visiting places

which subsequently host disasters. My daughter Liz visited the top of one of New York's twin towers just months before the terrorist planes razed them to the ground. And she spent her honeymoon in the Maldives shortly before the devastating tsunami struck. If you're thinking of going on holiday to some far-flung outpost, check with Liz first!

Most players' only reason for venturing beyond the confines of their hotel was to meet up with some local senorita who had caught their eye on a previous visit and taken their phone number! Yet in hindsight I bet those players who have now retired wish they had taken a little more time to admire sights of the tourist variety.

Our experience with Jimmy Adamson in Malta reminds me of the time Leeds were playing at Newcastle and Don Revie was a stickler for punctuality. Two reporters had accompanied the team on the bus from Leeds—Yours Truly and Phil Brown, a bald, ageing Sports Editor from the *Yorkshire Evening Post*. Phil had covered Leeds United since dinosaurs roamed the earth, or so it seemed, and was still doing the occasional match before retiring and handing over the writing duties to his much younger successor, Don Warters.

Phil had a lovely dry sense of humour but he could be a grumpy beggar at times and he wasn't in the best of moods because he hated covering matches at St James's Park. In those days to reach the press box you had to climb a spiral staircase that seemed to go on forever. That was bad enough for Phil, but the box was sited on a stand roof and he had long since worked out that the only means of escape in case of fire and a blocked staircase was to throw himself out of the press box into the crowd far below!

Thankfully that eventuality never happened but on this particular occasion Phil had something else to complain about. He had been delayed dictating his final batch of copy. The result was that we were late reporting to the team bus, which was nowhere to be seen. As we were not there at the appointed time, Revie had decided to leave us behind, doubtless reasoning that we wouldn't make the same mistake again. I'll never forget the oaths that flowed from Phil when he realised we faced catching a train to York and a long wait for the connection to Leeds.

Phil had some strange tastes in eating establishments. Whether it was to save money on expenses I don't know, but he would always seek out his favourite 'greasy spoon' café— the dingier the better. Knowing that he wasn't exactly accustomed to dining a-la-posh, I was amazed to see him berate the staff in York station's less than fashionable refreshment room because his tea and pork pie were only lukewarm. In fact he went one step further by throwing the offending beverage all over the floor and telling the horrified staff to clean it up. Hell hath no fury like a veteran newspaper reporter left behind by the team bus!

Phil was in at the start of United's European travels and he knew all the pitfalls which reporting from behind the Iron Curtain entailed—especially the problems of telephone communications and censorship. We had to be careful not to offend the home team and officials, otherwise reports would be heavily censored. The weather, too, could be a challenge and Phil enjoyed telling the tale of how he was so cold during a match in Leipzig that ice left the telephone sticking to his ear. I had my own problems when United went to Romania to play University Craiova in the seventies.

The journey involved a flight from Manchester to Bucharest, followed by a short domestic flight to Craiova. That journey from Bucharest was a real nerve-jangler. The plane was a rubber-band job and, if we were not already nervous enough, we were told an 18-year-old on his first commercial flight as a pilot was flying it. Judging by the bumpy ride I wouldn't question that information for one moment. A further concern was the heat ominously coming from the floor of the aircraft. My feet were almost frying by the time we touched down and I swear if our journey had been much longer that plane would have burst into flames.

The flight was an omen for the whole trip. Craiova was a miserable place, with poor food and hotels. From a distance it wasn't possible to tell whether the shops were open or closed because they were all dimly lit by 40 watt bulbs. I felt mightily relieved to be born west of the Berlin wall because this was Communism in the raw.

Everywhere we went the KGB secret police followed, their trilbies and long raincoats betraying any attempt to disguise their occupation. Our itinerary included a reception at the University during which we tasted the local firewater and were obliged to drink countless toasts to everything and everybody until we could hardly stand. The match kicked off in the afternoon, which meant the *Telegraph & Argus* could carry a report in its final edition that day. All seemed well when I was shown to my press box seat which had a telephone perched on the writing surface. I had arranged for my office to call me every 15 minutes during the match, but when the first call failed to arrive I was slightly concerned. When the phone still refused to ring, half an hour into the game, and I was told I couldn't dial out, I began to panic.

Eventually I discovered my calls had been coming through but on a telephone in the secretary's office two floors below! By the time calls switched to my phone in the press box the second half was underway and I discovered a colleague back in Bradford at the *Telegraph & Argus* had taken details of the first half from a live broadcast on BBC Radio Leeds. Inevitably the spellings of the Romanian players' names were well wide of the mark and, as the report carried my name, I just had to hope readers wouldn't notice the errors. At least when I arrived home and read the report, the spellings of the Leeds players' names were correct!

These days, most reporters send their copy from laptops,

thereby avoiding those potential disasters when copytakers miss-hear the words being dictated. I can assure you there was nothing more frustrating in the hurried world of sports journalism than getting a copytaker who, even at the height of Billy Bremner's fame, had never heard of him and insisted on having his name spelt out three times before moving on to the next name on the team sheet. It was the equivalent of some present-day copytaker asking how to spell David Beckham's name!

A fast, accurate copytaker is worth his or her weight in gold and before the advent of the laptop I often hung up the phone when I knew the worst copytaker in the *Telegraph & Argus* office was on the other end of the line. I never claimed to be the best sportswriter in the world, by a long chalk, but I always tried to do the job to the best of my ability.

I remember being a young reporter and being told by a much more senior colleague never to read my own report in the Saturday pink or it would ruin my weekend. What sound advice that was. Readers, managers and players are rarely aware that reporters don't write their own headlines. That job is performed by a sub-editor in the office and at the 'pink' the role was often filled by people who were news sub-editors during the week. Many of them had no interest in sport whatsoever, but they enjoyed pocketing the extra cash for doing a Saturday shift on the 'pink'.

A good headline can make a story and any journo worth his salt gets the main point of the tale into the first paragraph (known as the intro). It should guide the sub-editor to the desired headline. Sadly, some of the news subs at the *Telegraph & Argus* were led to water but wouldn't drink. The instance I always use to illustrate how a good story can be ruined by a bad headline dates back to a game at Bristol City where that rugged defender Norman Hunter was playing against his old club Leeds United. I was covering the game for the 'pink' and, after five minutes, Leeds striker Ray

Hankin had a goal disallowed. Bristol went on to win the game 4–3 with, of all people, Norman Hunter scoring the winning goal.

Naturally I led off my story on the lines that Norman had sunk his old club with a rare goal. Imagine my chagrin on arriving back home to pick up the 'pink' and reading the headline: 'Leeds get unlucky on a no-goal'. To me, that ranks as the worst sports headline in history and when I discovered the identity of the offending sub-editor I gave him both barrels when I confronted him at the office on the Monday morning. I was later made to feel guilty, as the guy was nearing retirement and my protestations were so severe that he took ill and had to go home to recover! Fortunately for him and me, he never sub-edited my copy again.

On another occasion at Bristol City's Ashton Gate a thick fog descended on the ground for Leeds' visit, but the referee ill-advisedly decided play could start. As player identification was almost impossible, my report was full of references to ghostly figures flitting in and out of the gloom—that sort of stuff. At half time the referee sensibly decided to call the game off, so I rang the sub-editor in the office and suggested he scrap the copy I had already sent and I would replace it with an updated story based on the postponement and news of when the match was likely to be played. My suggestion was greeted with something less than indifference by the inconvenienced sub-editor who would have been perfectly happy to use my original version, with the match-off decision in the last paragraph, so he could make an early departure for home!

Some of the most enjoyable social events during my time at the *Telegraph & Argus* were the Bradford Press Golf Circle matches against clubs in the paper's large circulation area. A round of golf against our readers afforded an opportunity for feedback about the paper's content and, as well as enjoying the courtesy of the course, Press Circle members were treated to a complimentary meal. New friendships were made and, although the standard of golf among some of the assembled hacks left much to be desired, our hosts' hospitality and patience never wavered. The press team ranged from low handicap club members, who played several times a week, to those like me who loved the game but found little time to play and carried a high handicap.

It was purely down to that high handicap that I managed to win the Bradford Press Golf Circle Winter League in the days when I tended to use little more than a three iron, nine iron and putter! That three iron received so much use—off the tees and fairways—that during one round at Thornton Golf Club, it snapped in half, much to my embarrassment and annoyance. I had the shaft replaced but it was never the same club again.

I didn't get around to reporting on golf, but those writers who covered the major tournaments at that time assured me it was a sportswriter's dream. Not only did they get to travel the world, but they were treated royally by tournament sponsors and returned home weighed down with freebies. One golf writer on a major regional paper took great delight in telling his envious friends how Dunlop provided him with a brand new set of tyres for his car. Not bad for simply doing his job!

One of our least proficient golfers was a guy called Phil Kelly. Phil was the kind of character who left us never knowing whether to laugh or cry. When his name appeared in a team it was a relief that you wouldn't finish up with your side's worst score, but knew you might as well be a man short! Slight of build and looking like a man well into his seventies, he had a face suggesting a life spent knocking back too much Scotch and smoking too many Woodbines.

On or off the golf course he was rarely seen without a fag dangling from the edge of his mouth—and how that cig would vibrate as he told many a fascinating tale at great length. Phil had an opinion on everything under the sun, whether he was an expert on the subject or not. I shall always remember the time he attended a tournament at Moortown to watch his favourite professional, Seve Ballesteros. As luck would have it, Phil was relaxing in the golf club lounge, puffing on yet another of his cigs, when in walked his hero Seve, who had been practising on the putting green. The unsuspecting Spanish genius made the mistake of sitting in the next chair, so we had arguably the world's worst golfer sitting alongside one of the world's greatest.

Phil wasn't going to miss this golden opportunity to strike up a conversation with the master. Leaving his fag in its usual precarious position and keeping a straight face, he nudged Seve on the forearm and, in all seriousness, said: 'Tell me, old boy, do you have trouble with your putts in the early morning dew?'

Seve took the question seriously and politely replied: 'Yes, I sometimes find it a problem.'

Without a moment's thought or feeling of inferiority, Phil butted in: 'So do I, old boy. So do I.'

6

MOONLIGHTING ON THE NATIONALS

Most journalists given the chance to work on national newspapers would jump at it. Fleet Street, in the days before the massive exit to soulless places like Canary Wharf, was the throbbing heart of journalism and for many hacks its pubs were an irresistible magnet. Yet despite a few offers, I decided to stay 'Up North' because I never fancied moving far from my roots. Most of my peers would have done almost anything for the chance to do my job—covering the mighty Leeds United.

Although I never moved to Fleet Street I did have the pleasure of working in the Manchester offices of the *Daily Mail* and the *Daily Express* as a casual sub-editor, and later freelancing for all the nationals. My stints at the *Mail* and *Express* were through financial necessity rather than ambition. I was working at the *Telegraph & Argus* when the National Union of Journalists (NUJ) called members in Newspaper Society offices out on strike. Even though I had paid into the Union's coffers from the moment I became a newspaperman at the *Pudsey and Stanningley News*, there was no strike pay.

The strike was called in the middle of a particularly cold winter and I remember doing picket duty, shivering outside the *Telegraph & Argus* offices in the centre of Bradford before making my way to the local playhouse where a sympathetic member of staff dished out hot soup every lunch time.

The unions had an important part to play in most industries but in newspapers the printing unions were strong, while the NUJ was comparatively weak—so, as I've mentioned before, printers usually came out with much fatter pay packets than journalists. Our NUJ picket line was supposed to stop 'scab labour' and vital supplies like paper and newspaper ink from entering the building. Yet some of the more militant union members scored an own-goal with me by preventing me from collecting my wage!

Most of us didn't have our wages paid directly into a bank—we had to collect them from the accounts office where they were handed over in a small brown envelope by the accounts clerk, Eric Gambles, who treated the cash like his own. We were supposed to thank him profusely or he would remember and query our expenses the following week!

When we were called out on strike I forgot to pick up my wage, so the next day I tried to enter the building to obtain what was owed to me, only to be prevented by my fellow union members. Despite my protests that I was only going to collect my wage and had no intention of becoming a 'scab', the pickets would have none of it. So much for unions standing up for their members' rights.

One particularly prosperous member of the *Telegraph & Argus* staff, who had been instrumental in leading us out on strike, found a way of cashing in by transferring his savings into the accounts of his children so he could draw social security money. We all secretly hoped his kids would abscond with the cash but unfortunately, and through misplaced loyalty, they never did.

The rest of us had to find employment of any kind or starve as the strike wore on and I was lucky to obtain shifts at the Manchester offices of the *Mail* and the *Express* because the national newspapers were not involved in the strike. I had immense respect for the expertise of those national newspaper journalists and the experience gained during my casual shifts was worth even more than the considerable payment I received. In fact, I enjoyed those shifts so much that I continued doing them long after the strike was over, even though it meant a full day's work at the *Telegraph & Argus*, followed by a dash over the Pennines to Manchester to work on the nationals.

If the *Telegraph & Argus* had found out that I was moonlighting, I suspect my P45 would have been in the post, but with a hefty mortgage to pay and a young family to support, the risk seemed worthwhile, especially as I had been offered permanent employment at the *Express*.

The drive to Manchester and back over the M62 motorway was often hazardous in winter and I remember one especially scary journey home. I was about three-quarters of the way through a shift at the *Mail* when I looked outside and saw huge flakes of snow descending on the street outside. Knowing I faced that journey home over the M62, northern Sports Editor Brian Webster kindly told me I could leave early and it was just as well because my vehicle was one of the last allowed on to the motorway before the slip-road near Manchester closed.

How I got home that night I'll never know as cars and lorries all around me skidded and stopped in the drifting snow. One of my spark plugs kept misfiring, presumably affected by the damp, and I knew that on the steep incline out of Lancashire into Yorkshire if my car stopped I wouldn't be able to restart it. Miraculously I kept going but the snow was almost as bad in Leeds and when I arrived at the entrance to the housing estate where I live in Horsforth, I realised there was no way I could drive through the drifts to reach my house.

There was no alternative to abandoning the car, along with all the others which littered the side of the road, and trying to collect it the next morning. When I trudged through the snow the next day it was clear I would need assistance. Fortunately,

Leeds United legend Norman Hunter, who lives round the corner from me, spotted my predicament and offered a much needed helping hand. Norman may have been a fearsome character on the field for Leeds and England but he has always been a gentleman off it and as amiable a character as you could wish to meet. My, was I glad to see him that morning!

Eventually I was driving into Manchester for another of those shifts when I noticed an advertising poster, part of which read: Are you killing yourself? To this day I don't know what that poster was advertising, though I suspect it was an anti-smoking campaign. I took it as a warning that if I continued to work all hours my health would suffer, so I ditched those trips across the Pennines and, for the time being, contented myself with covering Leeds United for the *Telegraph & Argus*.

My decision to reject an offer to work full time for the *Express* was one I never regretted, especially after the Manchester offices of the nationals closed. Not that the opportunity to work for other prominent papers disappeared. From my days on the *Pudsey and Stanningley News* I had freelanced for the now defunct *London Evening News* as their Leeds United correspondent. The chief sports reporter for the *Evening News* was Victor Railton, doyen of football writers in the capital at that time, though he unnerved me by calling me 'love' and 'sweetie' when ordering match reports! I covered Leeds United's matches for the *Evening News* whenever a London side visited Elland Road and I'll admit to getting a kick out of knowing my reports were being read by so many in the capital. Later I freelanced for the *Evening News*'s rival, the *Evening Standard*, and I relished having a picture by-lined diary piece every night during the week leading up to Leeds' FA Cup final against Sunderland in 1973.

United infamously lost that game to Ian Porterfield's goal, but a year earlier, Billy Bremner and his men lifted the famous trophy for the first and only time. It was Wembley's centenary final and Allan Clarke's headed goal from Mick Jones's cross sank old rivals Arsenal. I was on the team coach on both occasions and I wouldn't have traded places with anyone, contrasting though the results of the two games were. Strangely, though I wasn't even playing, I felt the butterflies in my stomach on the morning of both matches because I was so close to the players. It seemed bizarre sitting in the lounge of the Hendon Hall Hotel on Cup Final day watching pre-recorded televised interviews with players who were just a few feet away from me as they viewed themselves on the screen. Manager Don Revie was renowned for his superstitions and, as the team coach made its way to Wembley, Don was convinced the sight of a bride on her way to church was a lucky omen. Leeds had been bridesmaids so often in a football sense—now they were to be brides.

The celebration at London's Café Royal, after the victory over the Gunners, went ahead without the players who, ludicrously, were ordered by the Football League to play a title-decider at Wolverhampton on the Monday. The FA Cup took pride of place at the banquet and there was a comical moment when United chairman Ald. Percy Woodward invited anyone in the audience to 'Come up and have a touch!'

United lost their Championship decider at Wolves, handing the title to Derby, and no-one will convince me that the then Football League secretary Alan Hardaker wasn't delighted. Hardaker and Don Revie had been arch enemies for years and whenever Leeds needed help with their congested fixture list, Hardaker seemed to take immense delight in rejecting their pleas.

Whether it was the excitement of the Wembley victory or simply through eating and drinking too much, I was struck down with the galloping trots on the journey from London to Wolverhampton. Much to Don Revie's annoyance, the players' amusement and my embarrassment, the team coach had to make an extra stop so I could rush to a service station's toilet. It was not until some years later that the team coach had its own loo and, in the meantime, I remember big Leeds striker Ray Hankin having to pee in a bucket on the journey home from one away trip, having sunk countless cans of beer.

I wrote earlier in this book about headlines making or ruining a story and I am indebted to my former *Telegraph & Argus* colleague Brian Smith for coming up with the pink's headline for the Wembley victory: Clarke nods and it's United's cup at last. Brian had the happy knack of summing things up in a few well chosen words and I thought his headline succeeded in doing exactly that.

My wife Helen travelled to Wembley with the players' wives and thoroughly enjoyed the trip. Unfortunately, she has no interest in football and turned up resplendent in a red and white trouser suit—Arsenal's colours! Bless her. The few reporters who travelled with United in the late sixties and early seventies were made to feel part of the club by Don Revie who sent a telegram to my home when Elizabeth, the first of our two daughters, was born. Similarly, a telegram arrived from Brian Clough's successor Jimmy Armfield when Louise arrived on the scene. Christmas cards signed by Don Revie and subsequent managers arrived every year and I suppose I could make a packet if I chose to sell them—not that I ever would.

When Johnny Giles and Jimmy Armfield left the club they sent me letters of appreciation for my coverage of the club and I still cherish those letters. Brian Clough, of course, didn't stay long enough at Elland Road to be in charge at Christmas but his arch enemy Revie would have stood more chance of receiving a card from him than me! The public perception of Don was that he was a rather dour character, intensely superstitious and obsessed with winning at all costs. Perfectly true, but he also had a keen sense of humour. On one occasion Leeds were due to play at Portsmouth and we stayed at a hotel on nearby Hayling Island.

Herbert Warner was a jovial character who always accompanied us on away trips. A jeweller, who sold many of his wares to the players at knockdown prices, Herbie, as he was affectionately known, was chiefly responsible for calling out the numbers at the players' bingo sessions. He sometimes wore a ludicrous wig and was the butt of the players' jokes, but he didn't care—and Don sensibly encouraged him to keep team spirits high. The hotel on Hayling Island was a classy joint and the players, Don and the press decided to play a trick on Herbie who had a habit of taking home those small jam and marmalade jars from the breakfast table.

As usual, Herbie had stuffed his pockets with the things, not realising we were about to shop him to the hotel's management. With the help of myself and others, club captain Billy Bremner obtained a letterhead and we typed a warning letter purporting to be from the hotel manager. It read:

Dear Mr Warner, It has come to my attention that you have been stealing items from the breakfast table at our hotel. I cannot over-emphasise the seriousness of this behaviour and I have informed your manager, Mr Don Revie, that if it happens again I shall have no alternative but to ban Leeds United from staying with us in the future.

Herbie fell for the ruse hook, line and sinker. Distraught and ashamed, he sought out Don Revie and apologised profusely for any embarrassment caused and pleaded not to be banned from future travel with the team. It was only when the coach was pulling away towards Portsmouth that Billy, Don and the team owned up, burst into laughter and Herbie was the most relieved man on the South Coast.

7

DOOR-STEPPING ERIC CANTONA

There are many benefits and privileges attached to being a sportswriter. I long since lost count of the matches I've covered since becoming a journalist, but the figure must run well into the thousands and, of course, I've never had to pay to watch a match when working.

As an example of how out of touch I am with the cost of watching football, I visited Oakwell with my future son-in-law Tim and one of his pals to watch Barnsley play a league game during the 2005–06 season. Feeling unusually generous for a Yorkshireman, I offered to pay for all three of us as we arrived at the turnstiles. When I pulled out a £20 note, everyone, including the gateman, burst out laughing. 'Where's tha bin for t' last 30 years?' the gateman asked.

I hadn't the time or the inclination to explain, so I just pulled out another £20 and it still wasn't enough. Free travel, whether on team coaches or car journeys, free food and drink and free newspapers—these are just some of the perks sportswriters quite rightly take for granted.

When anyone asks if I pay to watch football when I'm covering matches for newspapers I simply ask them if they have to pay to carry out their line of work. You see, most people—and that includes some newspaper employers— don't rate sports writing as work. They think of it as a hobby enjoyed by those who do it, hence the poor rates of pay and long hours worked in many cases.

When I was covering Leeds United for the *Telegraph & Argus*, The National Union of Journalists carried out a survey among provincial journalists of hours worked in a particular week. Mine totted up to 140 hours and it wasn't an unusual seven days. Many is the time I started work in the Bradford office at 8.30am, covered a match that night, maybe on the South Coast, and arrived home in the early hours, only to clock on again at 8.30am.

'If you don't like it, we can very quickly find someone else who does.' That was the standard response if we dared to ask for a pay rise or more time off. Of course we enjoy the work most of the time, or we wouldn't do it for a living, but the problem is that everyone seems to think he or she can do the job. Now I don't profess to be any good as a plumber and I'm sure I'd blow up countless electrical items if I tried my hand at the electrician's trade. So what makes people who have never been near a newspaper office or a journalism course, think they can do the job properly?

In the early days of local radio I remember a freelance journalist in the north east blowing a fuse when a schoolteacher arrived in the Hartlepool press box to cover a match for the local station. The journalist had received some training before taking up the mike and was happy doing the job in addition to his newspaper work. The pay wasn't particularly good but it was a useful addition to his income—until the schoolteacher arrived and announced that he knew the radio station's Sports Editor very well and had been told he could cover Hartlepool's matches in future.

The freelance was so angry that he asked the teacher: 'What time do you start school on Monday?'

Puzzled by the question, the teacher answered: 'Nine o'clock and the first lesson is woodwork. Why do you want to know?'

Back came the reply: 'Because I'll be there with my saw and spirit level ready to teach your class. How do you like that?'

On another occasion a market trader entered the same press box and was promptly told to expect an extra fruit and vegetables stall next to his own in future.

Sports writing has taken me to close-on 30 countries, including one memorable pre-season trip to Canada with Leeds United. We were based in Toronto—the bustling cosmopolitan city on the banks of Lake Ontario—and Leeds played just two friendly matches during our week-long stay. Sir Stanley Matthews coached one of the teams taking part and he greeted us like long lost sons because we were from England. What a gentleman he was.

Many years earlier, my grandfather had taken me to Blackpool's Bloomfield Road to see Stanley play and at a later training session I gathered the autographs of the entire team that won the FA Cup at Wembley in 1953—the Matthews Final. What I'd give to know where that autograph book is now! Although those two matches in sunny Toronto were supposed to be friendlies, one of them took an unexpectedly nasty turn when a striker who played for a team from Ecuador tripped over fresh air as Leeds' Trevor Cherry moved in to challenge him. When the player's outrageous claim to a penalty was refused, he chased referee Gordon Arrowsmith, a Toronto policeman, bringing him to his knees with an attack from behind.

As the entire Ecuadorean team, substitutes and officials rushed on to the pitch and besieged the referee, the match was abandoned, with tempers on the boil. The indignant South Americans staged a sit-in, demanding a penalty competition to decide the match, but the Leeds players had already changed and manager Allan Clarke refused to take them back on to the pitch.

I quickly filed a report of the incident to the *Telegraph & Argus* and then the nationals back home and the proceeds paid for my spending money on the trip. We had plenty of time for sight-seeing, including a visit to the spectacular

Niagara Falls and a trip to the base of the Falls on the Maid of the Mist. Yet for every hour I've spent soaking up the sun in the company of football personalities, I've endured many more in draughty dressing room corridors or on windswept training grounds hanging around to interview players who would much rather be somewhere else.

Some players are happy to do interviews and take to the task like the proverbial ducks to water, while others will use any excuse to dodge a waiting hack. Harry Kewell's favourite ruse was to hold his mobile phone to his ear and wander past journalists as he pretended to be engaged in a long, vitally important conversation. You had to hope Harry was in the mood to do an interview or you had no chance. Mind you, there was one occasion when I thought he had dodged me by using the mobile phone routine when, on reaching the other end of the players' car park, he put the phone in his pocket and shouted after me: 'I thought you wanted to do that interview. What are we waiting for?'

Footballers just love to surprise journalists and get the upper hand if they can. To this day Paul Reaney, the former Leeds and England right back, has a wicked sense of fun. When an injury kept Paul out of one particular match at Elland Road, his replacement was a young defender called Nigel Davey. I thought the lad had a promising debut and afterwards I bumped into Paul in the club car park.

'What did you think to that kid who took my place,' he asked in a sneering voice, hoping I would pull the lad's performance to pieces. Fortunately, I gave an honest assessment and told Paul I thought the lad had done very well.

'I'm glad you said that,' he grinned, 'because I want to introduce you to his parents who are standing right here next to me.'

Duncan McKenzie was an impish exhibitionist who thrived on being interviewed and, like Paul Reaney, remains a good friend. Duncan was one of Brian Clough's buys during those chaotic 44 days in charge at Leeds and the talented striker stayed on after Clough's abrupt sacking. Among Duncan's many talents was an ability to jump over a Morris Mini car from a standing start and to throw a golf ball the length of a football pitch. He loved publicity and would emerge from the dressing room after matches, make a bee-line for the assembled press and cheerily ask, 'Now then lads, what would you like to know?' Ten minutes later my notebook was full of fascinating quotes.

Flamboyant former England international striker Frank Worthington was one of the game's true characters. The self-confessed playboy, who went on to write the appropriately entitled book *One Hump Or Two?*, joined Leeds from Birmingham City in March, 1982, staying until December of that year. He scored some spectacular goals but couldn't save the club from relegation under Allan Clarke's management. Frank, who had been a legend at Huddersfield Town, became a good friend of mine at Leeds and, like so many of his fans, I admired the footballing tricks that seemed to come so naturally to him. I like those big name footballers who don't take themselves too seriously and Frank was—and still is—such a man. Taking on the appearance of a rock star, he would often turn up for training looking like he hadn't shaved for days. I well remember Frank walking from his car towards the players' entrance wearing a tatty black leather waistcoat and matching trousers. I couldn't help calling after him that he'd missed emptying one of the club's dustbins! Fortunately, Frank appreciated the joke and laughed it off.

Another close friend of the media was Ian Rush, the former Liverpool and Wales goal machine, signed for Leeds by Howard Wilkinson on a free transfer in May, 1996. Rushie stayed at Elland Road for 15 months before George Graham parted with him and he became affectionately known as 'Rent A Quote'. You could question Ian on any topic involving football and he would talk forever if you let him. Ask him one question and he would answer half a dozen. If only most footballers were like Duncan McKenzie and Ian Rush, especially nowadays when interviews are very rarely done off the cuff and you have to go through a press officer if you wish to speak to a player.

Big name though he undoubtedly was, Eric Cantona proved to be an obliging interviewee during his time at Leeds. The Frenchman never spoke to me in riddles about seagulls following trawlers, and I suspect he appreciated my decision to take an interpreter along with me from Leeds University whenever I wanted to interview him. During his time in Leeds, Eric rented a modest semi-detached house in Talbot Gardens, Roundhay, a stone's throw from Allerton Grange Comprehensive School, where I was a pupil many years earlier.

On the day Eric left Leeds United to join Manchester United, the *Daily Express* asked me to camp outside his house in the hope of landing an exclusive interview. Although his dirty boots were left outside his front door, unnoticed by a procession of passing school kids, Eric failed to show up. He had gone to ground and I had a wasted day—apart from the sizeable pay cheque for my door-stepping session.

The *Express* man who commissioned my door-stepping of Eric's house was Phil Osborn, a pugnacious little man with a boxer's nose. Phil, who knew his job inside out, operated the northern sports desk at the *Express* in London after the Manchester office closed and he was a stickler for detail. He had a gift for getting straight to the point of a story and ensuring every line of enquiry had been exhausted. Sometimes his attention to detail was irritating, especially when he insisted on telling me to go back to my source for more info, but he was right most of the time.

One of my daily tasks was to phone Phil and tell him what story/stories to expect from me. He would write them on his schedule for the Editor's conference and I am certain there were times when he didn't care whether I followed through by delivering all the stories. So long as they appeared on his schedule, Phil could satisfy the Editor that there would be no shortage of tales that day.

When asked to name the best 11 Leeds players I've seen I don't include Eric Cantona because it was only after leaving Elland Road for Manchester United that he reached his true potential. Inevitably, my selection chiefly comprises players from Don Revie's 'Super Leeds' side and I make no apologies for that. In the old formation, I go for Martyn; Reaney, Madeley; Bremner, Charles, Hunter; Lorimer, Clarke, Jones, Collins, E. Gray.

John Charles was equally at home at centre back or centre forward but I've selected him at the back so I can keep the best smash and grab duo in the business together—Allan Clarke and Mick Jones. I've cheated a bit with Charles because, apart from watching vintage black and white film, I've never seen him play competitively, but I am well aware of his glowing reputation for Leeds and Wales and I once had the honour of playing alongside the 'Gentle Giant' in a charity match at Guiseley. It was long after John's retirement but he could still head a ball harder than most players could shoot!

Nigel Martyn was a superb shot-stopper, right back Paul Reaney had the extraordinary knack of keeping George Best quiet and made so many goal-line clearances that he was known as the club's third goal post. Paul Madeley, Revie's 'Rolls Royce' had to get in my team somewhere and with the supremely gifted Eddie Gray filling the left wing berth, Paul fills in at left back. The incomparable Billy Bremner is an automatic choice in the half-back line, along with Norman 'Bites Yer Legs' Hunter. It's a pity there isn't room for Gordon Strachan but Peter Lorimer scored so many goals from the right wing that he gets the nod. Similarly I wanted to include Johnny Giles but wee Bobby Collins just shaded Johnny as the club's best midfield general. I reckon that team would be more than a match for any side in the world.

One of the drawbacks to life in the press box is the need to maintain a certain decorum when your team scores. To be honest I've never been one of those excitable types who goes delirious when the ball billows the opposition's net. Self control has rarely been a problem for me—though I will admit to 'losing it' when Allan Clarke scored what proved to be the winner against Arsenal at Wembley in 1972.

I well remember Don Revie's 'Super Leeds' team going down to a totally unexpected FA Cup fifth round defeat at Colchester in 1971 and I'll never forget the reaction of the local scribes. The enclosed press box was packed to capacity for this classic David and Goliath tie. Colchester won 3–2 and every time the home team scored, the local reporters jumped up from their seats in excitement, banging their heads on the press box roof. Doubtless they were too enthralled by what was going on out on the pitch to feel the pain.

We reporters are supposed to be unbiased, but there was a guy called Keith McNee who covered Burnley, the love of his life, for many years. Keith stopped short of wearing a claret and blue scarf and rosette on working days, but no-one was left in any doubt as to his loyalties. Whenever I arrived in the Turf Moor press box with Don Warters from the *Yorkshire Evening Post* and Barry Foster from the *Yorkshire Post*, Keith would invariably greet us with the words: 'Ah, here they are again, the Yorkshire mafia.'

I well remember that uncompromising Leeds defender Norman Hunter committing the first foul—as he always did—at Turf Moor, and the indignant McNee promptly standing up in the press box and bellowing for all to hear: 'A leopard never changes its spots!'

Keith would certainly have been at home working for a local radio station these days when all semblance of unbiased reporting seems to have disappeared. BBC Radio Leeds, who cover the West Yorkshire area, even use separate commentators and summarisers for derbies between teams on their patch, with the commentaries on different wavelengths. The two sets of fans can listen to the match from their own perspective—and that's how they like it.

8

GOOD AND BAD LUCK

(Meeting Jimmy Armfield and missing a call from Vinnie Jones)

If there's one thing in life that is as important as good health it has to be good luck. Every sportsman needs it and so does every sportswriter.

To a certain extent, of course, we make our own luck by cultivating contacts and trying to be in the right place at the right time, but there are occasions when a stroke of good fortune and good timing comes out of the blue. A classic case to illustrate my point was the exclusive I gleaned from Jimmy Armfield on the day the former England captain succeeded Brian Clough as Leeds manager. Although Jimmy had been Bolton's boss for three years, he lived in his beloved Blackpool where he was a legend after playing over 600 games for the Tangerines, as well as winning 43 England caps.

Jimmy still lives in the North West Coast resort but, now in his seventies, he has been diagnosed with throat cancer. At the time of writing this book, I am able to use the title of Gentleman Jim's own first book and say he is 'Fighting Back'. That the Big C should strike one of the most universally liked men in football is a classic case of how unfair life can be at times. Thankfully, the medical experts say the prognosis is good and I hope they are right because Jimmy has remained a true friend long after leaving Leeds United and joining the media. You could always be sure his pieces in the *Daily Express* were accurate and the opinions he still expresses on Radio Five Live are based on sound common sense and the experience of a lifetime in football.

As luck would have it, I was spending a holiday at my grandparents' home in Blackpool, just a mile or two from Jimmy's home near Squires Gate, when news filtered through that he had landed the Leeds job. Good timing or bad? Should I continue my holiday and keep my head down or should I attempt an interview? Being young and enthusiastic I didn't think twice. A quick call to a contact on the *Lancashire Evening Gazette*'s sports desk provided me with Jimmy's phone number and, after a brief conversation with his charming wife Anne to discover the couple's address, I was round there like a shot.

Anne met me at the door of the couple's bungalow, invited me in and asked whether I preferred tea or coffee. Jimmy was asleep on the sofa but it wasn't long before he woke to find this journalist, notebook and pen poised, waiting for an interview. It was one of the most informal chats I've had with a football manager and, after ensuring I had all the information I needed, Jimmy asked me if I'd like to accompany him on the 80-mile drive to Leeds for their match against Arsenal on the Saturday.

I needed no second invitation, of course, and duly reported to his home on the morning of the game before travelling over the Pennines in his maroon Rover to the Mansion Hotel, Roundhay, on the outskirts of Leeds. That's where the players were having their pre-match meal and, as we pulled into the car park, we were met by a posse of familiar faces among the photographers and reporters who must have wondered why I was in Jimmy's car!

The newly appointed manager introduced himself to the players, though he wasn't due to take charge officially until the Monday. He watched the game, which Leeds won 2–0, and as we left via the ground's main entrance we were almost in collision with a passing motorcyclist! Imagine the headlines if Jimmy had been involved in a crash on his first visit to

Elland Road since his appointment! Having narrowly avoided the motorcyclist we continued our journey back to Blackpool where I continued what was left of my holiday, having first obtained Jimmy's views on his newly inherited team.

The following April, Leeds were preparing for the second leg of a European Cup semi-final in Barcelona when I dropped in on Jimmy at the team's hotel for a few quotes. After the business part of the conversation, Jim lit up his pipe and said: 'When you came round to our house in Blackpool I bet you never thought we would be sitting here, six months later, just one game away from a European Cup final.' You bet I didn't, Jim.

Despite the absence of Peter Lorimer and Norman Hunter, who were left out of the team, Leeds defeated the mighty Barcelona 2–1 in the first leg of the semi-final. It was a memorable night at Elland Road where Billy Bremner and Allan Clarke scored the home goals and Juan Manuel Asensi's goal gave the Spaniards hope for the second leg at the Nou Camp. Barcelona had world class players like Johan Cruyff and Johan Neeskens in their ranks at the time. I remember thinking how incongruous it was that this team of such shimmering talents should base themselves at a modest hotel in Bradford and train on the pitch of local side Thackley during the build-up to the big game. What a culture shock it must have been.

Leeds drew the second leg 1–1 at the Nou Camp to reach the final, Peter Lorimer celebrating his recall with a goal and Dave Stewart playing the game of his life in goal after the 69th minute sending-off of Gordon McQueen. The big Scottish defender was reduced to tears in the dressing room after being sent for an early bath for swinging a punch at goal-scorer Clares, but Gordon was shedding tears of joy at the final whistle as United won 3–2 on aggregate to reach the final for the first and only time.

They went on to lose to the redoubtable Germans, Bayern Munich, at the Parc des Princes Stadium in Paris, victims of some very questionable refereeing. That's when I thought seriously about changing my job title from sportswriter to war correspondent. Leeds supporters at that time had a reputation for mayhem and the presence of horse-backed riot police inside the stadium was like the proverbial red rag to a bull. Fans went on the rampage inside and outside the stadium and, instead of having an enjoyable night on the town in Paris, I spent most of the night tracking down UEFA officials in the hope of discovering the punishment Leeds United could expect.

I was covering the match not only for the *Telegraph & Argus*, but the whole Westminster Press group, which had papers in many parts of the country. My call from the copytaker was due at 8am and I didn't crawl into bed until 6am. When I was awakened by the shrill noise of the telephone it dawned on me I had spent so much effort on the follow-up story that I hadn't had time to write my match report. After dictating the follow-up I then glanced at my notebook and sent my match verdict completely off the cuff. Thank goodness I was sober, unlike top national newspaper writer Alan Thompson who accompanied the press party on another trip into Europe. Alan worked for the *Daily Express* and was one of the most talented and popular sportswriters of his day, but he was fond of a drink or seven.

The match was played in the afternoon, so there was plenty of time for the guys from the nationals to return to the hotel and file their match reports from there. Unfortunately, there was also plenty of time to sink copious amounts of the local brew. When the phone rang in Alan's room he was much the worse for drink, sprawled semi-conscious on the floor and wearing only a tatty string vest—not a pretty sight I can assure you.

Those of his colleagues who had anticipated the problem managed to bring him round and, unbelievably, he proceeded to dictate a word-perfect, thoroughly accurate account of the match in perfect *Daily Express* style. It wasn't a method I would recommend to any budding sportswriter, though I must confess I marvelled at that particular miracle.

When going abroad, whether on business or holiday, it's advisable to learn a few phrases of the lingo, of course, but Thommo, as he was affectionately known to colleagues and readers alike, was more Yorkshire than a Yorkshire Pud. Not for him long nights studying a Spanish phrase book. His approach was simply to stick the letter O on the end of English words and hope for the best. So he would ask a waiter for 'steako and chipso', or if he preferred fish, and the waiter didn't understand 'fisho', he would simply shout louder and extend the word to 'feeeeeesh'. No wonder we English are frowned upon as lazy.

Thommo was a hugely gifted journalist, as was his close friend from the *Daily Mail*, Bill Mallinson. When Thommo and Mally were around you were often left to follow up their exclusive stories. Their contacts were second to none and both had an excellent turn of phrase. Together they ran the northern journalists' golf day, which was not surprisingly sponsored by a whisky company and played on the pair's home course at Fixby, Huddersfield. Thommo and Mally knew every blade of grass on that course and they invariably carried off gallons of whisky as prize-winners. No-one resented their plunder as they always worked tirelessly to organise the event.

Thommo's difficulty with foreign languages reminds me that when I was at school they taught us Russian. It was around the time of the Cuba crisis, when it seemed Russia and America were about to blow the world into eternity. I am ashamed to say I remember just two sentences of Russian. One means 'You are not a good girl' and the other translates into 'I do not speak Russian!'

The importance of timing—or to be more precise bad timing—dawned on me again when that remarkable character Vinnie Jones signed for Leeds from Wimbledon. Hoping to catch Vinnie on his home telephone before he set out for Leeds, I left a message on his answer-phone. Some time passed and I received no reply, so I set off for Elland Road in the hope of catching him there.

The journey proved a wild goose chase, so imagine my frustration on arriving home to be told by my wife Helen that Vinnie had phoned back soon after I'd left the house. Now I may have mentioned previously that Helen has not the slightest interest in football and at that time Vinnie hadn't made it big as a Hollywood actor either. So the conversation went something like this:

Vinnie: 'Hello, is John Wray there please?'

Helen: 'No, he's gone out to meet some footballer Leeds have just signed.'

Vinnie: 'Yes, that's me, I'm the footballer. Vinnie Jones is the name.'

Helen: 'Oh, I'm sorry, I had no idea. I'll tell John you phoned when he gets back. Where are you from?'

Vinnie: 'Well, I play for Wimbledon but I live in Hertfordshire. What's it like living up north?'

Helen: 'Oh there are some lovely places to live...'

Half an hour later the conversation ended. Helen had been chatting away to Vinnie about houses, parks, shops, eating places and just about every topic you can name except football—and I missed my exclusive.

Vinnie had a reputation for taking no prisoners on the football field but for most of his time at Leeds he was on his best behaviour, much to the relief of referees! Some Leeds fans, on the other hand, continued to give journalists the kind of headlines that boomed out after the mayhem in Paris many years earlier. The situation had become so serious for the club by 1984 that director Maxwell Holmes, who was adept at pleading Leeds United's case at a succession of Football Association hearings into crowd violence, wrote to the Home Secretary pleading for stiffer sentences for offenders.

I managed to obtain a copy of the reply which read:

The Home Secretary has asked me to thank you for your letter of 23 October about the sentencing of football hooligans. As Mrs Pallett explained in her letter last year, the Home Secretary cannot seek to direct the courts in sentencing offenders. Earlier this year, however, sentencing guidance was given to the lower courts by the Court of Appeal.

Delivering the Court's judgment in a case involving violence at a match, Lord Justice Lawton said that in cases involving violence at or near football grounds, sentences must deter future violence and, in the absence of mitigating circumstances, youths between 17 and 21 should receive custodial sentences for offences involving violence to the police or to bystanders.

He also indicated that deterrence should be a consideration in the sentencing of young offenders. The Government certainly endorses that view, and reports from the police of cases following matches where serious incidents have occurred indicate that magistrates are prepared to take a serious view of such offences.

You will also be aware that the Department of the Environment recently published a report by an official working group which had examined what further steps might be taken to tackle the problem of football hooliganism. They are now consulting a whole range of interested bodies—including, of course, the football authorities—about the working group's proposals.

Yours sincerely, Christine Heald.

Fine words indeed, but football hooliganism was to continue besmirching Leeds United's name for some years after that letter was penned. Leeds still have a big following away from home despite the club's slide down the divisions, but thankfully the fans' behaviour has improved beyond recognition. Fewer stories for journalists, yes, but the safety of spectators at our football grounds has to be welcomed and applauded.

9

AGONY AND JOY
OF THE MISPRINT

Misprints and cock-ups in general are guaranteed to infuriate journalists and amuse readers. Before new technology, newspapers were produced on linotype machines by printers who were often paid by the number of lines of metal type they set. There were no penalties for mistakes and, with deadlines vitally important, speed tended to be at the expense of accuracy. There was nothing more galling for a writer than to see a carefully crafted story appear littered with literals, with his or her name at the top. Saturday night sports papers were especially vulnerable, as they were rushed on to the streets within minutes of matches ending.

I've laughed many a time on reading that 'Jones scored with a prodigious 30-yard shit into the top corner of the net'. And I am convinced not every literal was accidental. Take, for instance, the news of Ray Illingworth's elevation to the England cricket captaincy soon after he left Yorkshire. The *Telegraph & Argus* front page story should have started: 'Ray Illingworth has been made captain of England after only three weeks as skipper of Leicestershire'. It actually read: 'Ray Illingworth has been made captain of England after only three **wees** as **sipper** of Leicestershire.

Then there were those headlines with a double meaning, like 'Roy Virgin's maiden hundred' or 'Mother of five in for the high jump'. There have been so many over the years that I wish I'd kept a cuttings book of all the gaffes. Here are a few examples collected by former *Yorkshire Sports* Editor C.R. 'Dick' Williamson and I swear they are all genuine:

E.W Swanton, of the *Daily Telegraph*: 'The ball lodged between his thighs and poor Virgin had to go.'

Yorkshire Post: 'The prodigious Stephen Warboys, who is 140 years and two months old, must now be a hot favourite to become the youngest boy ever to win a national junior title.'

Yorkshire Evening Post: 'Ball became 21 early this morning.'

Yorkshire Post: 'Both Old and Cooper, a well built 2 year-old, playing in only his second Championship match, made good use of a stiff breeze.'

Telegraph & Argus: 'In the 53rd minute Beech tried his luck from fully 335 yards but was well wide of the upright.'

Daily Telegraph: 'Paul kept his forwards well supplied with the ball and was ever willing to shoot himself.'

Press Association: 'Half time score: Blackpool 1 Everton 0. Full time score: Blackpool 0, Everton 0.'

Court case involving a Mr H.W. Mycock: 'Atkinson was alleged to have said on being charged: "The rotten swine won't give me a house. I have a knife. I am going to use it on Mycock."'

'Detective Ward said a number of elderly women were under the doctor.'

Headlines:
'I want more players—Dicks'.
'Nothing like a jump before breakfast to clear the head'.
'Dick takes up strategic position'.
'Hampton rises to the occasion'.
'Briggs ponced in a flash to find the gap'.

Stating the obvious:
'Honours even in 2–2 draw'.

Understatement:
Leeds scrape point at Anfield.

What a jumble:
If Jimmy Armfield had read one of my stories about him in the *Telegraph & Argus* he would have been perplexed to be called 'Jummy Armifled'.

Colourful:
Jimmy's home town club Blackpool were colourful in more ways than one when they had a forward line comprising Green, White and Brown—no misprint, I promise.

Two of a kind:
There was a nightmare situation for journalists covering Leeds United's home game against Crewe Alexandra in February, 2008, when the Railwaymen turned up with two Gary Roberts in their team. Both men played in midfield and neither had a middle name, so the only method of identification was their different ages or mentioning that one Gary Roberts was on loan from Ipswich Town.

There are far fewer misprints these days as journalists set their own stories on computers, with linotype machines long since sent for scrap. And with sub-editors and reporters much more streetwise, there are fewer chances of those unintentional innuendos slipping through.

My old *Pudsey and Stanningley News* Editor, Eric Gooseman, wrote the headlines on all the paper's news stories and I'll never forget one of his 'masterpieces' of alliteration about a local supermarket called Fine Fayre which had fallen foul of the fresh food regulations. Whether the alliteration was intentional or not I'll never know but the headline read: 'Fine Fayre fined fifty pounds for unfit fish paste'. Ronnie Barker's stuttering character Arkwright would have spent an eternity trying to read out that little gem.

Then there was the picture which appeared on the front page of the *Pudsey and Stanningley News* and had schoolboys and little old ladies giggling for days. Amateur fruit and veg. growers in the area delighted in displaying their tomatoes, apples, giant marrows and cauliflowers etc at annual shows and the *Pudsey and Stanningley News* photographer was always there to snap the winners. On this occasion the winner of the cucumber competition was photographed with his magnificent vegetable in an unfortunate erect position and the caption read: 'Mr Joe Lightowler displays his prize specimen.'

Sport is full of clichés, of course, and it's easy to fall into the trap. How many times have you read the headline: 'Jones stakes his claim', or 'England look to bounce back?' Managers, coaches and players speak in clichés all the time and the current favourite buzz word is 'hopefully'. If I had a fiver for every time an interviewee had started to answer a question with 'hopefully', I could write off the national debt. 'Hopefully we'll get the right result. Hopefully we'll climb the table. Hopefully I'll be fit inside a month. Hopefully we'll reach the next round. Hopefully the manager will strengthen the squad. Hopefully the ref will admit his mistake. Hopefully the fans will get behind us. Hopefully the chairman will be patient. Hopefully I'll be selected to play. Hopefully...'

When readers of the *Telegraph & Argus* and *Yorkshire Evening Post* opened their newspapers during Bill Fotherby's chairmanship they must have thought the headlines were misprints. Fotherby, a firm believer that publicity was good for the club, would try anything to get punters through the turnstiles. When he telephoned me at the *Telegraph & Argus* and Don Warters at the *Yorkshire Evening Post* to say Leeds were hoping to sign the Argentine international Maradona, infamous for his 'Hand of God' goal against England in the World Cup, we thought he was joking.

Of course the transfer never took place—Leeds had more chance of signing super-star singer Madonna—but it made front page news for both papers once Fotherby had persuaded us he was serious. Bill was, and still is, a larger than life character and a dead ringer for Ted Bovis, the portly comedian from the TV holiday camp series *Hi-De-Hi!* Bill signed up many a sponsor for Leeds United and his boundless energy and enthusiasm are now being enjoyed by Harrogate Town where he is chairman.

When misprints occur, they are especially galling if they appear under your by-line, but since I went freelance, most of my reports in the national press are accompanied by a pseudonym or a gash by-line, as it is known in the trade. When match reports are, of necessity, hard-hitting, I am glad of the anonymity, despite the honesty of my sentiments. Yet I've written under so many different names that when the newspapers arrive at home, Helen often asks: 'So who am I married to today?'

Newspapers have long had a list of in-house names which they place on copy received from freelances. It is therefore common to see a report appear, word for word, in several newspapers under different names. That's fine when the sub-editor knows which gash by-line has been used on a specific match report. Then he can use different names on other reports. Unfortunately, identical made-up names sometimes appear on different match reports in the same edition. Even in these days of fast transport, it's impossible for a journalist to be at two matches at the same time!

I was amused when the *Daily Sport* and *Sunday Sport* used to use the by-line Ray Johns on my reports. It didn't take a genius for those who knew me to work out that John Wray was Ray Johns. So that particular pseudonym was dropped. Unlike television journalists, who are instantly recognisable, most newspaper and radio journalists can go about their daily lives unrecognised. When I went along to a local bonfire with my family it was fascinating to overhear two football fans comparing my reporting with that of a journalist on a rival paper. They had no idea I was there and fortunately their comments were favourable, otherwise there could have been an embarrassing confrontation!

It was an education to hear their views because it's easy for a sports journalist to lose touch with what his readers are thinking, especially as most people who take the trouble to write to newspapers have an axe to grind. Given the opportunity, I am sure it would be a worthwhile exercise for sports journalists to mingle with the crowd once in a while. As well as learning a few choice words, they may pick up some useful ideas for future articles.

In my present job with Gosnay's Sports Agency I take many phone calls on Saturday nights from representatives of local clubs keen to have their results printed in the papers we supply. Most are thoroughly reliable and we are indebted to them for that. A few, however, are inclined to spend so much time at the bar that they think it's a wheeze to sneak a cheeky name or two past us and into print. In the cricket season I've regularly been told a certain F. Ough has scored runs. A rugby union secretary tried unsuccessfully to fool us with the name P. Enis, while some ass insisted one of his footballers was called D. Obbin. All very amusing, of course, but a minefield for the unsuspecting journo on the other end of the phone!

10

CONSCIENCE AND THE *DAILY SPORT*

It's hard to call yourself a Christian when you freelance for the *Daily Sport*. Yet I am and I do. When I chose to leave the *Telegraph & Argus* in 1990 and join the long established Gosnay's Sports Agency, I never suspected that one of our customers would become a newspaper packed with topless models, mucky stories and adverts for sexual favours. I'm no prude, but when I attend my local Baptist church every Sunday it isn't wise to examine too closely where some of my income comes from. Not that I've ever written anything other than sport for that particular paper—previews of Leeds United matches, sports news items and reports on football and rugby matches are my remit—honest.

Yet I will admit to experiencing pangs of conscience whenever a newspaper boy or girl delivers the *Daily Sport* along with the other national newspapers, so I can check whether our agency's stories have been used. Sometimes the *Daily Sport* fails to arrive and I suspect giggling kids are reading it avidly on their way to school. I hope it does them no harm, especially when considering how easy it is for young people to obtain adult material these days, but maybe I should make the effort to collect the *Daily Sport* from my local newsagent in future.

Many years ago, when alcoholic drinks were served in the press room at Elland Road, there was a barman who had a penchant for collecting blue films which he was encouraged by some journalists to show before matches. They were pretty tame by today's standards and club officials had no idea that they were being shown behind the bar. That is until one offended journo from one of the quality Sunday papers wrote a vitriolic article roundly condemning the peep and giggle shows. They came to a rapid halt once the cat was out of the bag.

I would never call myself a religious fanatic, but I do believe that if you attempt to live your life according to Christian principles you won't go far wrong. You probably won't make a fortune because success in business sometimes calls for harsh decisions which can adversely affect people's lives and livelihoods, but I believe it is possible to combine being a sports journalist with Christianity. Until I first attended Lister Hill Baptist Church in Horsforth, about 15 years ago, I hadn't been near a church since leaving junior school, apart from getting married and attending the occasional funeral, but the Rev. Graham Banks preached a sermon that was to turn my Sunday morning routine on its head. I had never met Graham, but my wife Helen was asked to go along to Lister Hill to exhibit at a craft fair. Someone at the fair then invited her to church and I accompanied her, not exactly kicking and screaming but wishing I could have spent an extra couple of hours in bed.

Graham had no idea that I was in the congregation that morning, and he knew nothing of my job covering Leeds United or that I grew up in Bramley, Leeds, where I attended St Peter's Junior School and sang in the choir. He was just about to start his sermon when he stopped in his tracks and announced: 'I had something prepared but God has told me to cancel that and talk about some of the things I got up to as a lad in Bramley.'

If I thought preachers were aloof and out of touch with reality, Graham Banks blew my prejudices away in the next 25 amazing minutes. His early life almost exactly mirrored my own. He, too, was brought up in Bramley where he attended the same school and was caned by the same headmaster! Like me, he was repeatedly chased out of abandoned buildings which were an irresistible playground as they awaited demolition to make way for a new village centre.

He, too, had been admonished by the owner of a sweet shop at the top of Hough Lane for pinching gob-stoppers. And, best of all, he was an avid Leeds United supporter. I'm told Graham had never talked about his background in a sermon before that day and I can't recall him doing so again before leaving to become Minister of a Baptist church on the south coast. Call it co-incidence if you like, but I am convinced something much more spiritual was at work on that particular Sunday morning. Some years later, Helen and I were baptised—something I would never have countenanced before meeting Graham.

Mind you, there have been times when my journalistic work and membership of Lister Hill Baptist Church have clashed. Like the night I was belatedly asked by a national newspaper to file every word of a Dennis Wise press conference ASAP because they had a big hole to fill on one of the pages. With the newspaper's deadline rapidly approaching I was busy transcribing Dennis's wise words on to my laptop when the phone rang. 'Hello John,' said the caller in a cheery tone. 'A few of us have been discussing our preferred colour of new tiles for the gents' toilet at church and we would very much appreciate your thoughts.' How I resisted the temptation to tell the well-meaning caller to flush his head down the W.C. I'll never know.

Like many clubs, Leeds United have long had a chaplain to help the players with life's problems and there have been some staunch Christians in the dressing room, among them current Elland Road defender and Angolan international Rui Marques. Willie Bell, a defender who played in United's 1965 FA Cup final against Liverpool at Wembley, fills much of his time these days visiting British and American prisons to spread the gospel and his work has turned around the lives of many hardened criminals. Willie has a home in America but on one of his visits he agreed to do an interview with me for the club programme about his work with prisoners on both sides of the Atlantic. Some months later I received a letter enclosing a signed picture of Willie being presented to the Duke of Edinburgh before the Cup Final. Sadly, Liverpool won the match 2–1, watched by 100,000 people.

Gosnay's Sports Agency prides itself on being one of the most respected in the country—mainly because it has been a reliable source of sports copy since 1928. No agency survives for all those years by letting down contacts or customers. As a local agency we turn up at press conferences every week, so we can't afford to fall out with the players, managers, directors and coaches who are the source of our stories.

Most freelances try to meet the demands of the tabloids without betraying their contacts. Some make no attempt to bridge the gap and how they sleep at night I can't imagine. They may get away with it for a short while but eventually word gets around and they are no longer welcome at training grounds. I've always taken the view that no story, no matter how lucrative, is worth stitching someone up for—and this policy has stood me in good stead for many years.

Our agency was responsible for writing the Leeds United club programme for about 15 years until chairman Ken Bates decided to take the publication in-house through no fault of our own. Working on the match-day programme gave us unrivalled access to the players and management and we never abused that privilege. Unfortunately, two players, in particular, got the wrong end of the stick and accused me of sending stories to the tabloids when in fact a rival agency had 'lifted' those stories and passed them on to the nationals.

I wrote a feature on David Batty in the programme and towards the end of the piece David mentioned that when he played in the FA Cup final for Newcastle the players were below par for some reason and an indefinable something had been missing during the build-up to the game. A reporter from the rival agency read the piece and put his own spin on the story which he sold to a national paper. The headline was something like: 'Batty slams Newcastle "bottlers"'. At first David swore blind that I was responsible for the offending story and, even when I persuaded him otherwise, he refused to do any more interviews for the programme in case something similar happened. I could see his point, but it wasn't my fault.

On another occasion the then Leeds captain, Paul Butler, was interviewed by me and journalists from the *Yorkshire Evening Post* and the *Yorkshire Post* after a midweek evening match. We wanted some quotes for a preview story we were planning for the coming weekend's game against Watford. The story appeared in the *Evening Post* and the *Yorkshire Post* but I decided not to use it as I had a better tale in mind. Another agency lifted Paul's comments from the *Yorkshire Post* and sent them to the nationals with a slant which Paul didn't like. Because I had been in on the interview, Paul was perhaps understandably convinced the story in the nationals was mine. When I next saw him at the training ground he flew into a rage, telling me he would make sure none of the players spoke to me in future. I was livid and told him he was out of order. Now Paul is a big man and not the sort to mess with unless you felt you were the victim of gross injustice.

In the circumstances, I had no alternative but to complain to someone in authority so I furnished assistant manager Sam Ellis with the facts of the case. Big Sam had Paul in his office but I wasn't off the hook until I provided the club's press officer with the telephone numbers of the national papers' sports desks so they could obtain confirmation that the other agency filed the story. Paul was fine with me after that, which was just as well because one of my tasks was to ghost-write his column in the programme!

With so many websites, radio stations and other media outlets it is difficult to know where some stories have originated and the word 'exclusive' seems to have taken on a new meaning. It is especially galling to see stories appear in the nationals several days or even weeks after they have appeared locally. In fact, it's not unknown for the same story to appear in the same newspaper two days running if the guy in charge of sifting through journalists' copy is on a day off.

Deputies try to keep up with the recent content of their papers but they can't be expected to recall every story used. Some freelances take advantage of that and it's especially annoying when a brand new story of ours is kept out by someone else's tale that is so old it's covered in cobwebs.

In the higher leagues, the days when reporters rang the manager of the local football club at least once a day have all but disappeared and information is more often gleaned through press conferences, e-mailed press releases or official club websites. It is therefore much harder for freelances to obtain exclusive stories which won't be picked up by the nationals' staff men or the Press Association who regularly trawl clubs' official websites. Like many journalists of my generation, I am grateful for having lived through a time when the media and players were on first name terms, contacts were carefully cultivated and although reporters felt close to their local club, they never allowed themselves to be manipulated into following the party line to the detriment of objective reporting.

Unfortunately, some players and managers express opinions on the record and then try to claim they were misquoted when they read their comments in print. That problem has reared its ugly head many times in my career and I always feel let down by those who, on reflection, think their comments were ill-advised and then try to deny the words used were theirs. There have been times, of course, when interviewees **have** been misquoted and I remember

Howard Wilkinson falling out with a rival agency when they misrepresented his words in one of the 'red tops'. That particular agency had been covering news in and around Leeds but they fancied spreading their net to include sport.

Unfortunately for them, Howard knew and trusted our own agency and, after falling foul of the new guys on the block, he made it clear that ours was the only locally based agency he would work with. Howard had his critics but he was one of the most knowledgeable and thorough managers in football. He took Leeds to promotion from the old second division in 1990, guided them to the 1992 League Championship and, somewhat belatedly, the club have named a suite at Elland Road 'Howard's Way' in his honour. I always found him approachable and his quotes were rarely dull. In fact I used to accuse him of sitting up all night, dreaming up some of the metaphors and similes that cascaded from his lips. One of my favourites was his description of a hard task—'It's like pushing custard uphill'.

When Billy Bremner was Leeds' manager and the local press travelled with the team to away games, he would invite us into his office on our return—no matter how late at night. Then the wee man would pour us a glass of his favourite scotch and discuss the match from start to finish. Though we had our own views and expressed them in our match reports, we appreciated receiving that special insight from the manager—and he never complained about being misquoted. Happy days!

11

BANNED BY REVIE
FOR TWO DAYS!

If you are a sportswriter and you haven't been banned, you haven't lived. Such are the contrasting perspectives of club officials and journalists that no matter how hard you try to get along, sooner or later you'll fall out with someone if you are doing your job right.

I had daily telephone contact with Don Revie for many years and travelled with him and his team to many parts of this country and Europe. For the most part we got on famously, but even 'The Don' banned me for something he hadn't even read. Leeds were playing at Sheffield United in a Yorkshire derby and around that time Don had fallen foul of the Football Association for being over critical of referees. He was fiercely protective of his players who, as well as possessing admirable skills, had a reputation for taking no prisoners. Hence, referees tended to clamp down harder when they took charge of matches involving Don's team. He didn't like it, of course, and sometimes his comments led to appearances before the FA's disciplinarians.

I was covering the Sheffield game for the *Telegraph & Argus* and witnessed half a dozen Leeds players mobbing referee Bill Castle when he rejected an appeal for handball against Eddie Colquhoun as the Blades captain kept out Jack Charlton's shot. While Leeds were still arguing, Sheffield broke away and scored, compounding Revie's anger and that of his players. At the post-match press conference, the line of questioning from some journalists inevitably came round to Leeds players' behaviour. Don bristled and, rather unwisely, criticised the handling of the game by the referee. He fumed: 'It is all very well for people sitting in the press box to condemn my players for the way they behaved to Mr Castle. What you should remember is that our players had just seen two clear penalties denied them. I can well understand their feelings and actions. You should not be criticising them. The man you should be criticising is the man in black.'

That was the obvious story for the next night's paper and I filed it through to the *Telegraph & Argus*, making it clear that I felt Leeds' behaviour had done nothing to improve the club's image. Although the *Telegraph & Argus* is a Bradford newspaper, it had various selling points in the centre of Leeds. Don happened to be driving past one of these, near the City Railway Station. To his horror, he read the placard: 'Revie slams another ref.' Without stopping to buy a paper and read the offending story he rang the Editor at the time, Peter Harland, and told him: 'You can tell John Wray he is no longer welcome at Elland Road.'

Harland had me in his office in a trice and I must admit that his reluctance to fall out with Revie seemed to be clouding his journalistic judgment. He demanded to see my shorthand note of what Don had said and I duly obliged. 'Maybe you should have toned it down a bit, bearing in mind the trouble Don was already in with the FA,' I was told.

I felt let down by an Editor I had always held in high esteem until that moment. I felt I should have had his wholehearted backing—just as Ronald Crowther had from his Editor on the long-since defunct *Yorkshire Evening News*. Ronald, who later joined the *Daily Mail*, where he became that paper's top northern football writer, had upset the Leeds United board of directors with the tone of some of his reports. Eventually he was banned from the Elland Road press box, so instead he took his typewriter on to the ground's

Spion Kop and had a runner to rush his match reports to the nearest telephone. The club's ban failed to stop Ronald's reports appearing in the *Yorkshire Evening News* and the fans took his side against the board to a man. That episode brought Ronald to the attention of the national press and, excellent reporter though he already was, he knew the controversy helped him to land the job on the *Mail*.

Whereas Ronald's ban lasted for some time, mine was over in a couple of days. Don rang me and suggested we meet in his office where he explained that because he already had a disrepute charge to answer at the Football Association, he couldn't afford to be in more hot water with football's overlords, so he had to claim to have been misquoted. Like most of these disagreements, it was soon forgotten and Don brushed it under the carpet.

On another occasion, Dave Merrington, Jimmy Adamson's assistant when he was Leeds' manager, had me up against the wall of the Elland Road dressing room corridor for some minor misdemeanour. Obviously Dave didn't see it in those terms and I thought I was going to become a victim of GBH until he calmed down. Dave was an avid churchgoer and I wondered what the vicar or minister at his place of worship would have made of the undignified scene. I've met Dave a few times since and we've got on fine.

We Christians are as fallible as the next man, of course. We are all sinners who try to live our lives according to Christ's teachings but repeatedly fall short and ask for His forgiveness. Phil Rostron, who used to write for the *Yorkshire Evening Post* and became its Sports Editor before moving to another journalistic post in Carlisle, must have set a world record by being banned on his first day as the *Yorkshire Evening Post*'s specialist Leeds United writer. David O'Leary, who was then the club's manager, claimed he had been quoted on a remark that was supposed to be off the record—and he refused to speak to Phil on a daily basis after that. While I was writing this book, Leeds United withdrew all press facilities from the *Yorkshire Evening Post* after another disagreement between club and newspaper. In my experience neither side wins when a football club bans its local paper. The club receives less free publicity and is more likely to be criticised in print, while the paper is denied some of the exclusive stories which, under normal circumstances, would come its way. Eventually the *Yorkshire Evening Post* and the club settled their differences when the paper agreed to sponsor Leeds United's Members' Club.

Although I haven't been banned by Leeds chairman Ken Bates, I did find myself in the wrong place at the wrong time on attending the first press conference given by Dennis Wise on his appointment as manager. The conference was originally due to be held in Elland Road's Jack Charlton Suite, which involved going through two large wooden doors at the West Stand's main entrance. I arrived early and, on opening the doors, I was somewhat taken aback to be faced by Mr Bates and the club's media chief, Paul Dews, sitting on a sofa, waiting to go into the press conference at the appointed time. In fact the venue had been changed to the Billy Bremner Suite and 'Blaster' Bates boomed: 'Who let you in here? Our security is bloody terrible—but it's not as bad as our back four!' I had to laugh at that one.

The Jack Charlton Suite was the room where, over 10 years earlier, I had been recruited to the Football Association's Euro 96 team of press officers. The idea was that I would be responsible for publicising Euro 96, initially throughout Yorkshire but eventually concentrating on matches being staged at Elland Road. I was seconded from Gosnay's Sports Agency to the FA for more than a year leading up to Euro 96 and for several weeks afterwards for debriefing purposes. It was a fascinating experience, involving many trips to the FA's then headquarters at Lancaster Gate. It was a classic case of poacher turned

Don Revie faces the author to answer queries from Telegraph & Argus readers.

© Andrew Varley

Not so armless…Billy Bemner, the most inspirational captain in Leeds United's history, in the thick of the action.

Brian Clough and Bill Shankly lead out Leeds United and Liverpool before the 1974 FA Charity Shield at Wembley. Billy Bremner holds the League Championship trophy while Emlyn Hughes carries the FA Cup. Sadly the captains and managers are no longer with us.

Allan Clarke in typical pose, taking on a defender.

Cheer up, lads…Manager Jimmy Armfield (left) and coach Don Howe in pensive mood.

Peter (Hot-shot) Lorimer lines up the target as he shows the opposition a clean pair of heels.

Howard Wilkinson (centre) managed Leeds to promotion in 1990 and the League Championship in 1992.

Vinnie Jones…Not exactly Richard Burton but the hard man of Leeds' midfield went on to star in Hollywood

French genius Eric Cantona before his defection to Manchester United.

Football Association pass for the Euro 96 tournament and press tickets for some of Leeds United's big matches in Europe. The Spartak Moscow game was frozen off and later played in Sofia, Bulgaria.

Chairman Peter Ridsdale phones home from Moscow after Leeds' UEFA Cup third round, first leg, tie against Spartak is frozen off.

Eddie Gray talks tactics with Jonathan Woodgate (left) and Harry Kewell.

Manager Gary McAllister (right) and assistant Steve Staunton, who carry the hopes of present-day Leeds United fans.

gamekeeper and at my interview I remember the FA's media chief, David Davies, asking me what I would do if I came across a story that would show the FA in a bad light. It may not have been the most polished reply and I must confess at the time I thought I'd blown it and I still cringe when I remember it, but I blurted out: 'Well, David, you don't piss on your own doorstep.'

Fortunately everyone in the room saw the funny side, I got the job and threw myself wholeheartedly into getting Euro 96 as much media attention as I possibly could. For one match at Elland Road I needed a volunteer to don the costume for Euro 96 mascot Goaliath and walk round the pitch at half time. I was running out of possible 'victims' when Graham Banks, the then minister at Lister Hill Baptists, the church I attend in Horsforth, kindly put himself forward for the task.

When I revealed the identity of the man inside the costume, with his permission, it made a cracking story for the local press. Somewhat naively I had also arranged for my daughter Liz to dress up in Leeds United strip and accompany Graham round the pitch because it was difficult for him to see where he was going. I know I'm biased, but Liz was and still, is very attractive. Imagine the embarrassment caused to her and our Baptist minister when the crowd broke into a chant of 'Get your tits out for the lads.' Sorry Liz!

It was during Euro 96 that I met Angus Loughran, alias Statto, and to my shame I hadn't a clue who he was. I had an office in the media centre at Elland Road and Angus strolled up to my desk one day and handed me a very hefty file which I later discovered contained detailed stats on every player in the competition, as well as other invaluable background information. Having delivered the file, he turned round and left as quickly as he had arrived, and one of our young volunteers excitedly ran up to me and gasped: 'Don't you know who that was? Statto!' Presumably I should have been just as excited as that breathless volunteer.

Much to the relief of all concerned, and particularly officials of the Football Association, Euro 96 was hailed as an unqualified success. From a personal point of view it enabled me to take on the role of interviewee, after years of being an interviewer, and I must admit to getting a buzz from appearing 'live' on TV and radio as the FA's regional spokesman for the media. All the FA's press officers were well briefed during those countless visits to Lancaster Gate and I felt just like a politician fending off awkward questions, particularly about ticketing and pricing. I was also able to keep that promise to David Davies because, after witnessing a punch-up between Spain's bullish manager Javier Clemente and a press photographer—a story that could have earned me a lot of money from the tabloids—I ignored it. Naturally, the story came out when the photographer regaled his paper with the gory details, but at least my conscience was clear.

There were many enjoyable aspects to that job publicising Euro 96 and one of the best was attending a celebrity wine-tasting at a well-known Leeds city centre restaurant. The event had been organised by the *Yorkshire Evening Post* in conjunction with the restaurant owner who had agreed to supply wines from all the countries whose teams would be playing at Elland Road. One of my fellow tasters was actor Richard Thorp, who plays Alan Turner in *Emmerdale*, while former Leeds footballer John Hendrie was also on the panel.

The idea was that we would grade the various wines for tannin, nose and other technical terms used by genuine wine buffs. I always thought a nose was that hooter that starts between the eyes and usually ends just above the lips, but my lack of knowledge didn't stop me from enjoying the samples from bottle after bottle—and there was none of that spitting-out malarkey I can tell you!

Our pictures and comments duly appeared in the following night's *Yorkshire Evening Post* and I am indebted to the reporter who covered the progressively merry proceedings, Anne Patch, a former colleague on the *Pudsey & Stanningley News*, for turning my amateurish remarks into passable 'wine speak'. The tasting took place during late morning and I must have cut an amusing figure as I staggered back into Elland Road's media centre slurring my words and not exactly setting the right example to our student volunteers.

I started this chapter by remembering the time I was banned by Don Revie. I am pleased to say that was just a blip in our professional relationship and when Don died of motor neurone disease in May, 1989, I wrote the following obituary in the *Telegraph & Argus*:

Don Revie, whose motto during a glittering era of success as Leeds United's manager was a defiant 'Keep Fighting', lost his grim battle for life today. The former Leeds and England manager, whose name became synonymous with the club he dragged from obscurity to the forefront of world soccer, died aged 52 from motor neurone disease—the debilitating illness that killed Hollywood actor David Niven.

Revie made a desperate and tragically unsuccessful visit to Russia in search of a cure after his disease was confirmed by medical experts in America during the summer of 1987.

'It came as a tremendous shock to my family and myself,' he told me at the time. 'You can imagine the reaction when they said there was no cure'.

Don was nursed through his last faltering years by his wife Elsie at their retirement home in Kinross, Scotland. Before the illness virtually confined him to the house, he made a sentimental return to Elland Road, scene of countless triumphs during his 13 years in charge.

He received a tumultuous reception from over

25,000 spectators when he walked on to the field before United's game against Manchester City, the club where he gave his name to the Revie Plan—a highly successful version of the Hungarian deep-lying centre forward tactic.

Later he was to attend a special Elland Road game in his honour, but this time he cut a tragic wheelchair-bound figure as his terminal illness left him helpless.

Born in Middlesbrough, in 1927, Don played for Leicester City, Hull City, Manchester City, Sunderland, Leeds United and England, winning the Footballer of the Year accolade in 1955. Yet his appointment as Leeds' manager in 1961 happened by chance. Harry Reynolds, the then chairman, had recommended Revie to a Third Division club searching for a player-manager. But when Reynolds wrote out the glowing reference, he realised that if Revie was that good he should be in charge at Elland Road and the appointment was duly made.

Don was far from an instant hit in his new job. When he took over, United were ninth in the Second Division. They finished that season 14th and by February of the next season they were bottom, with Third Division football staring them in the face. They beat Newcastle 3–0 at St James's Park in their final game of the season to avoid the dreaded drop, and a new, exciting era in the club's history was about to dawn. Revie survived the catcalls and dwindling gates, built a side that took United to the Second Division title in 1964 and brought them undreamed-of success in the FA Cup, League Cup, First Division Championship, European Fairs Cup and UEFA Cup.

Manager of the Year three times, he was awarded the OBE and made Billy Bremner, Jack Charlton, Norman Hunter and the rest into household names. Although the Leeds side was initially criticised for being over-physical, even the club's harshest critics eventually confessed admiration for the richly talented 'Super Leeds' team which mesmerised opponents with breathtaking skill.

Perhaps inevitably, after his achievements at club level, Revie became England's Manager on Thursday, July 4, 1974, as successor to Sir Alf Ramsey, though Joe Mercer had a spell as caretaker-manager in between. Success eluded Don as an international boss, probably because he made too many team changes and missed the day-to-day involvement with his players.

The back door manner of his departure from the England job to become soccer supremo to the United Arab Emirates, on a four year contract worth £340,000 tax free, left a bitter taste. He was subsequently banned from taking any job in English football for 10 years. Though the ban was lifted on appeal, Don's image had suffered enormous harm and he later admitted regretting walking out on the England job.

After club posts in the Emirates and Egypt, he shook the sand off his sandals and was on the point of returning to English club management with Queens Park Rangers until negotiations broke down.

Whatever view you choose to take of Revie—brilliant tactician or cynical money grabber—no-one can deny his magnificent record which entitles him to rank among the greatest club managers of all time. Many have since tried to emulate his achievements without success—and the superbly equipped Elland Road stadium will remain a fitting monument to those glory years when Don Revie was king.

12

DEADLINES AND THE GO-SLOW LAPTOP

Match reporting facilities for the press have improved by leaps and bounds in recent years. The advent of laptop computers has forced those in charge of sporting venues to install power points—and some even have TV screens so reporters can watch action replays before compiling their descriptions. At many grounds, though, journalists must still rely on their first impression of how goals and tries are scored or runs made. Not an easy task if you are on the telephone at the time or your attention has been momentarily hijacked by an incident in the crowd or a colleague's conversation.

Many is the time I've had to rely on the guy sitting next to me to identify a goal-scorer or try-scorer, especially if the player's number was almost illegible. Playing surfaces have improved beyond recognition since the days when quagmires left players looking like mud-covered hippos. However, some clubs, especially those whose teams play in vertical stripes, could do more to improve the legibility of the players' numbers.

In football's Premiership, the problem is not so bad, as most players are household names, but outside the top sphere I wouldn't recognise the majority of footballers if I passed them in the street. I can only imagine that radio and television commentators spend hours poring over pictures of players from the teams they are about to cover. Those of us who used to confine our football or rugby reports to descriptions of the action must now compile laborious statistics which only stop short of the number of times a player has visited the toilet during the half time interval. Gambling companies need many of these stats, so punters can bet on anything from the number of shots on and off target to the percentage of possession enjoyed by each team. The task is particularly onerous at high-scoring rugby league matches where you are expected to inform the Press Association every time a try is scored or a goal is kicked, as well as keeping a record of substitutions, scrums, penalties and completed sets of tackles.

Friday night matches are the worst because they don't usually kick off until 8pm and national papers want reports sent immediately the match is over, if not before. In some cases there may be four or five reports to do, so I pray to God that my laptop or mobile phone doesn't let me down. When that laptop is on a go-slow, seconds can seem like minutes and every minute counts when meeting deadlines. I still have nightmares over a match report from Elland Road that fell foul of stringent deadlines because the modem connecting my phone and laptop refused to work.

Leeds had played Sheffield Wednesday in a Yorkshire derby and the *Mail on Sunday* required a 400 word match report on the whistle, followed by a 400 word re-write by 6pm, to include the two managers' quotes. I also had an order from a website for a match report of 400 words, plus a paragraph or two on the performance of every player who turned out in the match, including substitutes.

Also required were marks out of 10 for each player, a mark out of five for the referee, plus goal-scorers and goal times, details of bookings, dismissals, substitutions and the number of times each side hit the woodwork. Now that's some workload when electronic equipment is working perfectly, but when left with no alternative but to telephone the whole lot to copytakers, imagine the frustration and extra pressure involved.

I've always hated being late for anything, because I loathe letting people down, and late copy, no matter how rare, reflects badly on our agency. The relief, therefore, when everything works as it should, is immense. Electronic delivery of reports is now the norm and it's a far cry from the days when sportswriters used typewriters and handed their reports to 'runners' who would hurry to a telephone outside the press box, read the report over to a copytaker in the newspaper office and return for the next batch of copy from the journalist. I now use roving broadband to transmit my copy and it is both quick and reliable.

There is nothing football journalists hate more than a late goal that requires a hurried re-write with a deadline fast approaching. A classic case was the League One play-off semi-final, first leg, between Leeds United and Carlisle United at Elland Road in May, 2008. Carlisle were leading 2–0 and the referee decided there should be four minutes of added time. A full **six** minutes later, Leeds defender Paul Huntington, who was born in Carlisle, sent a high ball into the goalmouth of his home town club and striker Dougie Freedman snatched a goal for Leeds to give them a much-needed lifeline for the second leg at Carlisle three days later.

Until Freedman's last gasp goal I was ready to send my completed match report by e-mail at the touch of a button on my laptop's keyboard. The sudden turn of events meant not only re-writing the opening few paragraphs and changing the score-line but also checking through the rest of the report to remove Freedman's first name from subsequent copy, as naturally his full name now appeared in the intro. Accepted newspaper style is to use a player's first name once and thereafter refer to him by his surname.

More hasty re-writing was needed towards the end of Leeds' home game against Crewe in September, 2008. Leeds were coasting 5–0 in injury-time when defender Lubo Michalik was sent off. During Michalik's absence, Crewe scored twice! Although Leeds still won comfortably, the extra information which had to be included in my report caused an inevitable delay before I could file the copy.

One of my worst experiences at a rugby match happened in the early days of BBC local radio. While covering the Bramley Rugby League team for the *Pudsey and Stanningley News* I also did voice reports for BBC Radio Leeds. Bramley were playing their local rivals Hunslet at the latter's old Parkside ground and the press telephones were in a shed at the back of a stand. Not feeling confident enough in those early days to relay my post-match 'live' piece off the cuff, I made copious notes and had delivered the fourth paragraph of a 20 paragraph report when the lights in the shed went out. To my horror, I couldn't see my hand in front of my face, never mind my notes, so I had to entrust the remainder of the match to memory and complete the report which contained enough 'ers' and 'ums' to drive the programme's producer to near suicide.

Fortunately, I had time to drive into Leeds and re-record the report for Radio Leeds' teatime round-up of matches, but the 'live' debacle delivered on the final whistle was an all-time low in my career. Jim Brady, who had been a local newspaperman for some years, was Sports Editor of Radio Leeds at the time and he had an embarrassing moment of his own one evening. Leeds United were playing, Doug Lupton was the commentator and Jim was the link man in the studio. All was going well, with Doug in full voice, when suddenly the sound was lost. After a few seconds thousands of listeners heard Jim raging: 'Who the hell pulled that bloody plug out?'

More silence followed before Jim returned to the airwaves, having been told his angry comments had filled the airwaves, and announced: 'I'm very sorry everyone, but I'm still looking for the boody fool who pulled that plug.'

The press facilities at Elland Road have always been good. The press seats used to be directly behind the directors' box in the West Stand, so when visiting VIPs like the England manager or a big name from show-business were being entertained at the game you knew about it. Later, the press seats were moved to the rear of the stand and enclosed by glass. That made hearing the person on the other end of a telephone line much easier and it was far warmer for us in the middle of winter, but the atmosphere generated by the crowd was blocked out by the glass. So much so that it was impossible to hear announcements made over the public address system or chants from the crowd. The seats in that box were extremely comfortable and I half expected an usherette to come round selling ice creams, but I was pleased when the club decided to revert to having the press in rows of seats without any glass surrounding them.

One of the perks of being a sports reporter is the free food provided for the press by most clubs. Leeds United still put on sandwiches at half time and they used to serve a delicious hot meal before home games until Ken Bates suddenly, and without warning, ended the practice. It was said Ken took the decision on the grounds of economy, but an unsubstantiated rumour went the rounds that Mr Bates had taken umbrage after one journo complained in print that he had been refused an extra sausage! Reporters arrived at Leeds' home game against Birmingham in September, 2006, expecting the usual hot meal, only to be told of the chairman's economy drive. So some members of the media went out in search of a burger while others endured their hunger until the half time sandwiches. Those who were too busy working during the half time break simply went hungry.

Many of the hacks vowed to get their own back by filing less than complimentary match reports, but Mr Bates, as he so often does, had the last laugh. Leeds served up a delicious 3–2 win over Birmingham, the press ate humble pie and they reluctantly gave the team more toffee than they'd had all season. Sandwiches are now provided for the press before matches.

Although the authorities tell managers that they must attend post-match press conferences, journalists who need quotes often have to wait for players to emerge from the dressing room in the hope of catching a few words. Many clubs have a press officer who will endeavour to persuade a player or players of the media's choice to answer questions. In my early days as a football reporter, if you wanted players for a few quotes after a match it was always up to you to ask them and 99 per cent of the time they obliged.

There was one very embarrassing moment after a Leeds match at Tottenham when I wished I'd kept my mouth shut. There were far fewer black players around at that time and I wanted a word with a young Leeds prospect, Terry Connor, who was building a reputation with his home town club. After the match I made my way to the dressing room entrance and there was a player with his back to me. I tapped him on the shoulder and said 'Hello Terry.' A split second later he turned round and I immediately recognised him as the Tottenham player Garth Crooks who went on to become a well known TV presenter, of course. I blushed crimson, but Garth laughed it off and I don't suppose I was the first or last journo to make that kind of genuine mistake.

I was embarrassed again during an interview with Leeds defender Rui Marques before the first home game of the 2008–09 season, against Oldham. Usually, press conferences to publicise forthcoming matches are held at the club's Thorp Arch training ground, but because manager Gary McAllister wanted his players to train on the Elland Road pitch before the opening home game, the conference was switched to the stadium. Normally I make sure my mobile phone is switched off before a press conference, but on this occasion I totally forgot. Sod's Law decreed that when Rui was in full flow, I received an in-coming call which was heard loud and clear on local radio stations when the interview was broadcast.

Not that I was the only culprit that day. Many of Rui's

team-mates had gathered near the assembled media and thought it would be highly amusing to bellow 'encouraging' remarks to their long-suffering colleague such as 'boring, boring, boring'.

Sport does have its humorous moments but also its tragedies. The mood could hardly have been more sombre for those who attended the Bradford City fire in May, 1985, when 56 people perished and 265 sustained injuries. In the press box that day was a remarkable man. C.R. 'Dick' Williamson was long past retirement age, always wore a trilby and was still covering City's matches for the Press Association. A legend on northern grounds and far beyond, Dick had covered Bradford Park Avenue and Yorkshire County Cricket Club for many years and had been Sports Editor of Bradford's pink *Yorkshire Sports*.

When fire took hold of Valley Parade's main stand, many of Dick's colleagues feared for his safety when they couldn't find him. They needn't have worried. Dick had made his escape and hurried up the road to a public call box to file his account of that terrible day's events to the Press Association. His story went round the world and although he was naturally shocked, Dick escaped the inferno unharmed.

Only seen without that trilby if you happened to visit him at home, Dick was one of sports journalism's true characters who had a wicked sense of humour. He owned a seemingly never ending collection of fascinating sporting facts which he peddled for many years in a syndicated newspaper column. Long after his retirement he would wander into the *Telegraph & Argus* building to plunder facts from the newspaper's library and his cataloguing system was second to none. Ask him about any sporting fact and the odds were that Dick would come back with the answer long before the days of the internet. I had a Saturday night column on Leeds United when I wrote for the *Yorkshire Sports* and I often rang Dick for a relevant statistic to back up my arguments.

'Stick in a penny and out it rolls,' he would grin, as he duly turned up the information at the drop of a trilby. Mind you, if the Sports Editor of a national newspaper rang him for some obscure statistic, Dick would tell him how long it would take to sift through the files for an answer. In fact, he could glean the information in seconds, but by making the Sports Editor think immense research was required, the price went up!

Dick didn't suffer fools gladly and he would go for the jugular if you showed the remotest sign of weakness. Give as good as you got and you were his friend for life. I still chuckle over the fate of a young reporter who was sent to cover Yorkshire in a county cricket match at Scarborough. The youngster's self important manner in the press box irritated Dick, who decided to teach him a lesson. Despite his apparent self confidence the lad had trouble keeping up with events during the match and for the umpteenth time he asked: 'What happened then?'

In an instant Dick fed him the immortal line 'An all-run three' (how could you have anything but an all-run three?) The lad reported the all-run three without question and when Dick spotted it in that night's paper it brought a twinkle to his eye.

Williamson had an opinion on everybody and everything. He would argue for hours with anyone who took a different view and we had many heated debates on the merits and demerits of Don Revie whom Dick insisted on describing as 'that boss-eyed shyster from Middlesbrough.' It was a mild description by Dick's standards about a man he had never met! The politically correct brigade used to harangue the comedian Bernard Manning for his allegedly racist jokes. What they would have made of Dick Williamson I shudder to think. I am reliably informed that he regarded being a Catholic (left-footer in Dick's parlance) as the ultimate sin. Jimmy Scoular, the former Portsmouth, Newcastle and Bradford Park Avenue hard man, had a similar aversion to Catholics and it wasn't unknown for Jimmy to phone Dick during the days running up to a match to discover if there was a 'left-footer' in the opposition. On receiving confirmation from Williamson, Scoular would ensure his victim received an extra kick or two during the game!

Dick was a relentless critic of journalists who over-wrote, yet ironically he was one of the worst offenders for verbosity. If he could get his message across in 50 words he would use 500 to do so (payment by the word, you see). A typical Williamson piece would start: 'From the Arctic's icy wastes to the sandstorms of the African desert; from the gambling halls of Las Vegas to the penny arcades of Blackpool; from the towering Swiss mountains to the flatlands of the Netherlands—there is one baffling question no-one can answer—how comes it that England cannot find a footballer with the ability to stick a pig's bladder into the net?' Dick has long since passed on, but sports journalists in many parts of the country still revere his memory.

On the same day as the Bradford fire, I was reporting on Leeds United's match at Birmingham where a wall collapsed under the weight of the crowd, killing a young boy spectator. I was still shocked by that event when news of the Bradford fire filtered through to St Andrews. Those two tragedies certainly put the 'importance' of football into perspective as, of course, did the disasters at Hillsborough and Hysel. When a reporter turns up at a sporting event he doesn't expect to witness spectators carried out in body bags. How much worse, though, for those who lost loved ones in those tragedies. David Markham, a former colleague of mine on the *Telegraph & Argus*, was the paper's Bradford City reporter at the time of the Valley Parade fire. He knew many of the victims personally. David's red hair turned white overnight.

13

MIXING WITH THE STARS

At the height of Leeds United's powers, the team would stay at the country's swankiest hotels, many of them in London. The privilege of staying and dining at the Royal Garden Hotel, in Kensington High Street, was one of the perks and if memory serves me right the price of a modest room even back in the seventies topped £100. Naturally stars of the entertainment world frequented such establishments and I remember spotting impersonator Mike Yarwood, French singer Sasha Distell and comic Freddie Starr when they were at the zenith of their fame. Comedian Eric Morecambe was a huge fan of football and Luton Town, in particular, and I had the good fortune to meet him on the way home from Leeds United's European Cup semi-final in Barcelona.

When Eric spotted the Leeds party he began going through one of his hilarious routines and when he had finished he tipped his glasses in that trademark way of his, offered to shake my hand and, with immaculate timing, withdrew his hand just as I offered mine! Eric dissolved into a fit of giggles, though he must have played that trick hundreds of times on unsuspecting victims. Singer Ronnie Hilton, who had a string of hits in the fifties and sixties, occasionally travelled with us on the team coach and made recordings of some of Leeds United's best known songs.

Michael Parkinson and Trevor McDonald have been

among the big names whose work has taken them to Elland Road's press room, where everyone is treated alike, from the doyens of broadcasting and the written word to hospital radio commentators and journalists from obscure weekly publications.

I still have the vivid memory of Elton John arriving at the ground in a stretch limo for a match during the early days of his fame. He was wearing a fur coat and his hair was ginger, apart from sideburns which were dyed green. At the time he seemed like an alien from outer-space! When Batley Variety Club attracted entertainment's top names, some of them would take in a match at Elland Road—among them Shirley Bassey and Ronnie Corbett. John Cleese was another visitor, while in more recent times the club's training ground has hosted top band Kaiser Chiefs and Radio One DJ Chris Moyles, who are huge Leeds fans.

Nicky Byrne was a junior goalkeeper on Leeds United's books before finding fame with West Life, and when the singer visited the training ground to see his old pal Gary Kelly, his arrival sparked excitement in the O'Leary household. David O'Leary was United's manager at the time and his wife and daughter were huge fans of West Life. So when David phoned home to tell them Nicky had turned up they travelled over from their Harrogate home to meet the star.

Nicky couldn't resist joining in a training session and as soon as the singer had left the dressing room, Gary Kelly took his leather trousers off the peg, put them on and ran out to train in them, much to the amusement of the players and coaching staff. The renowned actor Kenneth Haigh was an avid Leeds supporter who would meet up with Don Revie and the team whenever they were staying in London before a match. Kenneth starred in a hugely popular TV series, *Man at the Top*, and after a long chat with him over a meal I wrote a piece in my weekly Leeds United column in the pink *Yorkshire Sports* under the headline: 'Man at the Top supports team at the top'.

The portly Paul Luty, who played the barman in that massively politically incorrect comedy series *Love Thy Neighbour*, was another regular visitor to The Royal Garden when Leeds were in town. We had to be on our best behaviour at such establishments, of course, and we needed to keep a close watch on our expenses. The price of food and drink was horrendous so sometimes the press would eat with the team, while other times we would find the nearest burger bar.

Footballers dined free, of course, and for some of them at the start of their careers, the opulence of London's top hotels was a real culture shock. Leeds-born Terry Connor had just broken into the first team as a teenager when he stayed at the Royal Garden for the first time. He glanced at the menu and couldn't believe his eyes when he saw the prices. Baffled by most of the offerings, Terry decided to play safe by ordering steak, medium-rare. When the meal arrived, the lad's steak was decidedly under-cooked. Calling the waiter over, he complained in his strong Leeds accent: 'Oi mate, take this back. It's still pumping blood!' The expression on the waiter's face was one of utter disdain, just as it was when I asked for a house wine instead of his much more expensive recommendation.

The story goes that some years later, one of Leeds' international midfield players was also eating at a posh London hotel. He had no hesitation in ordering tuna steak. Everyone began tucking in but there was a puzzled look on this particular player's face. Turning to the man next to him he complained: 'This steak doesn't half taste fishy, does yours?'

High class prostitutes frequented some top hotels in the capital and it was common to hear a knock at the door a few minutes after arriving back in your room. The assumption was that if you could afford to stay at such expensive hotels you could also afford to splash out on ladies of the night. To borrow a well worn phrase from the *News of the World*, I always made my excuses and declined in such circumstances—honest. Doubtless the players received similar knocks at their doors, though whether they succumbed to temptation I never found out.

Travelling with Leeds United meant basking in reflected glory in those days. Supporters would stare through the windows of the team coach in awe and when I got off the coach on our arrival at football grounds I was often mistaken for a footballer and asked for my autograph! For a long time I patiently explained that I wasn't a player, but in the end I just signed my name Mick Jones because we had a similar hair colour and were about the same height! Mick and I have laughed about that a few times since, but in hindsight it's not something I'm proud of doing. There must be lots of autograph hunters thinking they have a genuine Mick Jones signature from that era. If only they knew…

Mind you, not everyone was a Leeds fan by any means. In fact, there was considerable hostility shown to Don Revie's team by other clubs' supporters who were envious of Leeds' achievements. On leaving the grounds, Revie would advise us to pull down the blinds of the team coach for protection in case missiles came through the glass. On one journey we were heading towards the M1 motorway after a game at Queens Park Rangers when a brick came through the windscreen, narrowly missing the driver. Norman Hunter spotted the culprits and gave chase but even he couldn't catch them as they disappeared into a nearby housing estate. Fortunately, no-one was injured in the incident but the driver was in danger of frostbite as he drove over 200 miles with a shattered windscreen. Revie rewarded him with a sizeable tip for not delaying the team by waiting for a replacement coach.

Many of the London press hated Leeds and their manager—partly through southern bias and partly because they disapproved of the highly gifted team's reputation for winning at all costs. I remember taking my seat in the press box at a London ground and sitting alongside one of the big names from the national Sunday press. I couldn't help noticing he was scribbling away long before the game was due to start. His report was full of references to crunching challenges which had no place in a sporting arena and one of his phrases referred to Bremner's bone-jarring tackles causing sparks to fly from the pitch! That reporter didn't need a match. He had already decided to dip his pen in vitriol.

Our trips to and from away grounds were often spent playing cards or watching videos. Sometimes the manager would come over to where members of the press were sitting and tell us his team selection, or if we were heading home he would give us some quotes about the game or other topics. On the long trip from a match at Southampton in November, 1980, Allan Clarke, who was Leeds' manager at the time, provided me and two other local journalists with a cracking story. Clarke had issued 20,000 leaflets to Leeds fans at a game against Arsenal earlier that month, seeking their opinions on what was wrong with football in this country.

Several thousand replies were received, most of them highlighting hooliganism as the biggest factor keeping people away. Nothing unusual about that, you may think. But Allan astounded us by saying: 'Birching the thugs was among the suggested remedies and I agree. The louts who cause serious trouble at soccer matches are animals, so let's treat them like animals by birching them in front of the main stand at the next home match following their offence. If the law were changed to allow the birch, I would volunteer to join in the whipping on the pitch. That would really humiliate offenders. As managers we have to try and do our bit in the fight against crowd violence and our views should be heard.'

Allan was 34 at the time—the youngest manager in the old First Division. He was convinced his solution would be an effective deterrent but agreed there would have to be an enormous change in outlook by the authorities for the scheme to have any chance of being implemented. He added: 'The hooligans I want to deter are clearly out to cause bother no matter what happens on the field. Even the way they dress is intimidating. Extreme violence must be met with extreme measures.'

All three journalists on that coach made sure Allan wanted his controversial remarks printed before filing our copy. After the stories appeared, several reporters from the nationals rang him so they could write follow-up stories. To their surprise, he told them that although he stood by every word printed in the local press he didn't want his remarks appearing in the national papers. His attempt at suppressing the story stood no chance, of course, and it was duly run by the tabloids whose reporters lifted Allan's comments from our pieces.

Once a tale has appeared in the public domain, a manager has about as much chance of preventing it spreading as stopping an express train with his outstretched arm. I sympathised with Allan over that issue because he cared passionately about the club's image, which had been repeatedly tarnished by morons who were proud to be called hooligans.

Ken Bates was taken to task in many quarters for threatening to deal with Chelsea's hooligan fringe by electrifying fences at Stamford Bridge, though even 'Controversial Ken' can't have been serious about that one! Many sports personalities regret their words on seeing them in print and attempt to wriggle off the hook by claiming they've been misquoted. I have as little patience with that kind of behaviour as I have with those journalists who twist an interviewee's words to suit their own agenda.

It's a real privilege to rub shoulders with top sportsmen, many of whom enjoy careers in the media once they have retired—and why not? What would the television companies do without the likes of Gary Lineker, Alan Hansen, Andy

Gray, Sue Barker, Peter Alliss, Geoff Boycott, *et al*? Sportswriters with years of journalistic training and experience tend to resent top sportsmen being fast-tracked into roles as columnists or TV presenters. Dick Williamson, the former sports editor of *Yorkshire Sports*, had a splendid de-bunking column that was syndicated nationally. Dick repeatedly used it to harangue the BBC for spending what he regarded as huge chunks of the licence fee on unnecessary sports experts. Yet I've never subscribed to that view. Despite many years covering football, I, like the vast majority of sportswriters, lack the technical insight that past and present stars can bring to their analysis, though that shouldn't preclude me or any other sportswriter from having valid opinions to express, as I argued with Billy Bremner all those years ago.

Writing and television presenting call for different talents and I have always admired anyone able to slot effortlessly into either role once their sporting career is over. What I do object to are those ex professionals who are unable to string together more than two syllables but whose names figure at the top of ghost-written articles in newspapers and magazines. If the ghost-writer gets any recognition at all it is usually a barely noticeable tail-piece in six-point type. You can be sure the sports personality's fee will put the writer's pay cheque to shame, yet who does the bulk of the work?

The popular image of a footballer is someone with a low IQ who would be pulling pints or working on a building site if God hadn't blessed him with especially talented feet and an irresistible desire to succeed. Yet there are exceptions. People like Peter Lorimer and Johnny Giles were a pleasure to 'ghost'. More often than not they would have several topics in mind for their columns and, if they hadn't, they would warm to suggestions and effortlessly fill a notebook or tape recording.

Johnny is now a writer and broadcaster and a damned

good one too. On the other hand, there are those who either lack imagination or a willingness to co-operate, even if they are being handsomely paid for their columns. There's nothing worse than an interviewee who looks blank and answers questions with just one or two words. At times it's like pulling teeth and I begin to wonder whether working down a coal mine might be an easier occupation.

The next time you are watching a top sportsman being interviewed on TV, notice how rarely he looks into the interviewer's eyes. Often he'll stare into space and you get the distinct impression he would rather be somewhere else—anywhere else! I use the word 'sportsman' advisedly because in my experience sportswomen are almost always courteous and helpful. Good manners shouldn't take much effort. In fact, they should be a natural asset and in some cases they are. Yet too often those who get paid massive amounts for 'working' just a few hours a day shun the media who are, after all, there to ask questions on behalf of the spectators whose admission money helps to pay those massive salaries.

14

SENT TO INTERVIEW A FAMOUS CLASSMATE

Being a 'guinea-pig' can have disastrous consequences. Just ask those poor souls who volunteered for scientific experiments to test new products and almost lost their lives. I've been a guinea-pig, in vastly different circumstances, at least twice and although I started out with a degree of apprehension, the experience proved worthwhile. I am not proud to say that, while attending junior school in Bramley, Leeds, I failed my eleven-plus exam. If that had happened a year or so earlier I would have been written off as a dunce, possibly for the rest of my school life. Failing the eleven-plus in those days meant attending secondary modern school, with little prospect of landing a good job at the end of it, unless pupils passed a newly introduced thirteen-plus exam.

The brighter kids went to grammar school and were earmarked for university, leading to well paid occupations like accounting, banking and the legal profession. So it was little wonder that, when my parents opened that dreaded envelope to discover my eleven-plus failure, they were devastated. Yet, thanks to their concern for my future, they decided to move house to an area of Leeds where comprehensive education was in its infancy and pupils were handed an educational lifeline. At the time, I hated the idea of leaving working-class Bramley for the posh suburb of Moortown and I left my parents in no doubt about my feelings.

Fortunately, as things turned out, I had no choice in the matter and it was at Allerton Grange School where this guinea-pig became a late developer and a fan of comprehensive education. I had always enjoyed English as a subject but hated maths—a strange situation as my father was a tax inspector—and it was the dreaded maths that ruined my chances of passing the eleven-plus. At Allerton Grange, which had 1,500 pupils at the time, I was encouraged by a succession of excellent English teachers and my love of sport saw me represent the school at rugby, football, cross-country running and athletics.

Because the teaching was slower and there were more stimulating subjects than maths, I thoroughly enjoyed my time at Allerton Grange, where I passed my O- and A-level GCEs and was a classmate of Ian McGeechan, who went on to play for and coach the Scotland and British and Irish Lions Rugby Union teams. In fact, as I write, Ian has been appointed the British and Irish Lions coach for an unprecedented fourth time. Lions chairman Andy Irvine even hailed him as rugby's answer to Sir Alex Ferguson—a massive tribute by any standards. Ian played his club rugby at Headingley and has also coached club sides Northampton and Wasps. He is currently Wasps' Director of Rugby.

Irvine said: 'I see similarities between him and Alex Ferguson, I really do. His enthusiasm, his desire his intimate knowledge—there are a number of parallels. Ferguson's players love him, Geech's players love him. Geech is probably quieter. Alex Ferguson is probably more emotional, but both men's records speak for themselves.'

At school Ian was an all-round sportsman who could have gone on to play cricket for Yorkshire had rugby not been his first love. He moved to Allerton Grange from Moor Grange School where he had been head boy, and we played in the same rugby team at Allerton Grange where his talent was obvious to all. He was a supremely gifted centre or fly-half with exceptional pace, good handling skills and the eye for an opening. I was a slightly-built winger who thought he could run a bit but, in a friendly match which saw us on different sides, Ian gave me five yards start and still caught me with a flying tackle from behind.

Many years after our schooldays, I was sent by the *Telegraph & Argus* in March, 1990, to interview him at his home in Adel, Leeds, before Scotland were due to play England at Murrayfield on their way to the Grand Slam. I've interviewed countless big name sportsmen without being unnerved but I found it surreal quizzing someone who used to share the same classroom and play in the same school team. Ian and his wife Judith, who also attended Allerton Grange, could not have been more welcoming, and the interview produced a good piece, but I felt a strange tension that I am sure would not have existed had I simply called on Ian as an old school mate, rather than a journalist.

Allerton Grange pupils who attended the school long after I left included footballers David Batty and Brian Deane, who I interviewed many times when they played for Leeds United. In fact, Brian went out with my daughter Liz a few times before she met her husband Tim. Whether it was because I was Liz's dad I don't know—I always got on well with Brian on a professional basis—but he never came to our house. Instead he would park his car further along the road and call Liz on her mobile to let her know he was there!

Some players give their mobile phone numbers out to journalists and some don't. I didn't have Brian's until he phoned Liz at home one night and, when the call ended, I dialled 1471 to get his number. It was a bit underhand, I'll admit, but he never complained.

Unfortunately, David Batty will always be remembered for his World Cup penalty miss for England against Argentina, whereas he was one of the most reliable defensive midfielders in Leeds United's history as well as serving Blackburn Rovers and Newcastle United with distinction. Despite his considerable football achievements and the bright lights that attract so many top footballers, David was a home-loving family man who liked nothing better than playing with his twin sons and taking the family on holiday to caravan sites.

While I was a pupil at Allerton Grange I was taught history and general studies by a guy called Harry Patterson. That name will mean little or nothing to most readers, I'm sure, but Harry Patterson changed his name to Jack Higgins and became a best selling author who penned, among other classics, *The Eagle Has Landed*, which was turned into a blockbuster film. Harry, who eventually became a tax exile in Jersey, came across to most of his pupils as the original angry young man. It was plain, even in those days, that he was fiercely anti-American, believing most 'yanks' to be grossly incompetent, especially in warfare. That belief came over strongly in many of his gripping novels and I must admit that to this day, whenever I hear a newscast about Americans killing allied troops in so-called friendly fire, I bring Harry Patterson to mind and what he must be thinking.

Before he hit the big time, Harry was a struggling novelist who wrote in his spare time while eking out a living as a school teacher. He would moan to us about the publishers who had again rejected his novels so we never suspected we had a future best selling author in our midst.

In 2008, Allerton Grange made the national television news for all the wrong reasons when a youngster was stabbed by one of his fellow pupils. I never encountered that level of violence at the school, though I do remember a member of the teaching staff returning from his lunch break the worse for drink. He rather foolishly started picking on the tallest boy in the class who responded by delivering a stunning blow to the chin while the rest of us watched in disbelief. I never did discover what happened to the teacher or the pupil, though I imagine disciplinary measures were taken against both parties.

Serious violence in the classroom was a rarity in those days, thankfully, as we had it drilled into us by our parents that we must show teachers respect. And if I sound like Victor Meldrew I make no apologies!

Having left Allerton Grange and started my apprenticeship at the *Pudsey and Stanningley News* I became a 'guinea-pig' once again. They say there's no substitute for on-the-job experience and that's certainly true of journalism, but when the National Council for the Training of Journalists started block release courses, the *Pudsey and Stanningley News* management decided to enrol me on the first course to be held in the north—at Darlington College of Technology. It meant leaving home for two eight-week courses, which were held in the middle of winter, and I wasn't enthusiastic about the prospect at all. Leeds isn't the warmest place in the country, but Darlington's temperature is usually several degrees colder. This, allied to the prospect of returning to a classroom environment, left me fearing the worst. One of my reasons for rejecting the idea of going to college after A-levels was to start work and leave classrooms behind, yet here I was, reporting for lessons with 14 fellow cub reporters at Darlington Tech.

Eric Dobson, Editor of the *Newcastle Journal*, wrote in the course brochure:

The eyes of all who are concerned with the training of journalists are on this course, for its success will encourage the extension of this form of training which I regard as the best introduction to journalism of any yet devised. I wish you success on the course both for yourself—inasmuch as it will set you on the path to a notable career in journalism—and for the Press as a whole—for papers can only flourish if their staffs have the ability and the enthusiasm to match up to their responsibilities.

No pressure there then!

Because this was the college's first course in journalism, the staff were feeling their way. As I recall, only one had worked on a newspaper. Bill Wood had been news editor of the Shields Gazette and knew his subject inside out, but as far as I am aware the other lecturers had never been anywhere near a newsroom. The Pitman shorthand exercises were all geared to office dictation, so instead of taking down a shorthand note of a court case or a footballer's interview, for example, we did drills that tended to be based on business letters. It was almost as if we were training to be secretaries instead of reporters.

As I and some of the other students had taken and passed English Literature at A-level, it seemed a total waste of time to study the subject again, though the lessons on newspaper practice and newspaper law were very useful. Towards the end of the course we brought out a four-page tabloid paper called the *Northern Star* which can't have been bad because newspapers throughout the north-east plundered it for stories. As well as gaining writing practice we were encouraged to try our hand at sub-editing, including writing headlines. There were some excellent examples. One I particularly liked was 'Tattooists needled by scratchers', which appeared on a story about a Darlington tattoo artist who aimed to clean up the profession by ridding it of those inexperienced 'scratchers' who harmed their customers. Another story highlighted a shortage of barmaids in Darlington. The headline read: 'Barmaids in short measure'.

Apart from shorthand practice we didn't have much homework, so we spent most nights in the spit-and-belch pubs of Darlington where floors were covered in sawdust and we were introduced to the delights of Newcastle Exhibition beer. For those of us keen on football there were visits to the Feethams to watch Darlington who now have a new state of the art stadium on the outskirts of the town. The standard of football at the Feethams wasn't the highest by any means but watching the occasional football match was slightly preferable to getting drunk every night.

The highlight of our journalism course was a visit from one of the country's most famous comedians, Peter Cook, the tall part of the Peter Cook and Dudley Moore double act. Peter had a financial interest in the satirical magazine *Private Eye*, so he and Editor Richard Ingrams toured the north's universities and colleges to promote the magazine in an area of the country where circulation lagged behind London.

Cook had one of the sharpest brains in the entertainment business and he was as keen to learn more about our journalism course as we were to discover the latest secrets being uncovered by *Private Eye*. Like us, he had time on his hands at the end of the day, so he accompanied us to the local nightclub where we supped copious amounts of alcohol and exchanged stories before we staggered back to our student digs and he to his hotel. We also interviewed the great man for a piece in the *Northern Star*.

As I've said, there is no substitute for on-the-job training, but despite those 'wasted' English Literature lessons, those in authority declared the course a success and the *Northern Echo* plundered many of the stories contained in our course newspaper. Visits to the Tyne Tees TV studios and the offices of the *Newcastle Journal* and *Northern Echo* were among the highlights as they had immense relevance to media studies. Some of the best reporters I know never went near a classroom after leaving school. In fact many of them learned the job after starting out as tea boys or copy-runners—a career route closed to them these days. In my experience, some of the least competent journalists were fast-tracked into the business from universities without the grounding of five years on a weekly paper, for instance. They may have been able to chisel out an in-depth 'think-piece' or spend weeks researching a story, but ask them to cover a court case or meet a tight deadline from a football match and they were lost. Give me a sharp all-rounder any time above those award-winning specialist feature writers who rarely set foot outside an office, let alone meet the people they write about.

There seems to be an award for just about everything these days, including, I'm told, Loo of the Year. I'd happily flush most awards down the toilet, along with those has-beens who do the judging. And if you detect a note of jealousy, maybe you're right. On the other hand, I've never felt worthy of an award, so I've never entered for one—unlike those with time on their hands and egos the size of Canary Wharf.

15

WHEN BATH NIGHT MEANT A DRENCHING

Although I was a staff reporter for 26 years, freelancing was always in my blood. From the day I joined the *Pudsey and Stanningley News* as a junior reporter I was looking to earn extra cash by selling stories to regional and national newspapers. Many thousands of journalists have had good cause to thank the linage pool run by their papers with the full knowledge of the management. Linage is the practice of paying journalists by the line for stories sent to other newspapers. For instance, if there was a fire at Blackpool Pleasure Beach it would be of national interest, so journalists covering the story for the *West Lancashire Evening Gazette* in Blackpool would send the story to other newspapers who would pay for it.

The proceeds would be shared among the whole staff at the end of each month. The system was frowned upon by freelances who argued, quite rightly in my view now I am working on their side of the fence, that staff reporters are guaranteed a wage and should be content with that, whereas freelances need stories like a Pleasure Beach fire to earn their living.

Every area used to have a freelance agency which was protected by the National Union of Journalists from interlopers looking to make a quick buck by selling stories in their area. Now, it's open season, with reporters setting up as freelances after being made redundant by national and regional newspapers or leaving college without being able to land a job on a newspaper. The extra cash helps to supplement the former staff men's pensions or pay-offs and many a long-established freelance has been forced out of business because there is little loyalty shown by some newspapers to established agencies. I have known freelances having to wait over a year for their cash from newspapers who demanded that their stories were written to tight deadlines. What would a staff man's reaction be if he had to wait even a couple of months for his pay cheque?

Although there was no linage pool at the *Telegraph & Argus*, we were allowed to send stories to other newspapers within the group and my Leeds United copy was regularly syndicated. Unfortunately, one member of the *Telegraph & Argus* sports staff was envious of my extra income and I discovered through a third party that he had been complaining that I was earning money off the rest of the staff's back. His argument was that while I was taking my typewritten copy into the wire room to be transmitted to other papers, my colleagues were doing my work. It was a ludicrous argument, as I was away from my desk no longer than a couple of minutes and I would back my workload of writing and sub-editing for the *Telegraph & Argus* against anyone else's in the sports department at that time—as I told the whinger in no uncertain terms!

When I chose to leave the *Telegraph & Argus* in 1990 for Leeds-based Gosnay's Sports Agency, I was joining an organisation formed in the early part of the 20th century by, of all people, a High Court judge. William Gosnay decided there was a market for supplying football and rugby results to national and regional newspapers and he was absolutely right. Gosnay's office used to be a dingy hovel in the courtyard of The Golden Lion Hotel in Leeds city centre. Standing in the shadow of a railway viaduct, its walls would vibrate as steam trains, and later diesels, passed by on their way into and out of Leeds City Station. When someone took a bath in one of the hotel rooms, water would leak through the ceiling directly into the office, which was usually clouded in cigarette smoke. Wires led like spiders' webs from the ceiling to a host of black, old fashioned telephones which sat on a huge mahogany table. Drawers were opened not by handles but hooked pieces of string in this wonderfully atmospheric time warp and old newspapers piled high were an obvious fire hazard.

Because there was an understandable policy of taking care of the pennies so the pounds would look after themselves, buying notepaper was frowned upon unless strictly necessary. So when stationery levels were depleted, one of the partners would nip round to the nearby railway station and help himself to a stack of time-table handbills with a plain reverse so they could be written upon! Calls to newspapers were always done by reversing the charges, though most newspapers no longer accept such calls and even 0800 numbers are becoming rare. For more than 15 years, Gosnay's Sports Agency has been based in the Leeds suburb of Horsforth, avoiding those daily traffic jams into the city centre. We are not quite so frugal, though we do still take notes on the back of used sheets of paper. Old habits die hard, especially when Yorkshiremen can save money!

We are one of the longest established specialist sports agencies in the country, with many of our counterparts having gone to the wall. Gosnay's continue to supply match reports and sports stories to national and regional newspapers, but many of the local football results we used to send to the national papers have been hijacked by the Press Association, who obtain them from local leagues free of charge. Some leagues have remained loyal to us, as they value the publicity they have had from us over the years, and we thank them for their continued support, but we have had to look to new markets, such as websites and magazines, to replace lost business.

My mentors when I joined Gosnay's were Ray Oddy and Barry Wood, two highly professional journalists who, coincidentally, had also worked for the *Telegraph & Argus* in Bradford. When Barry left Bradford he joined the staff of the long since defunct *Daily Sketch*. Both were keen Rugby League men, though they turned their hand to every sport covered by the agency, and were well known and respected throughout the sports journalism industry. They have now retired but I owe them an immense debt for the knowledge they passed on to me and the freelancing career opportunity they gave me.

Barry still lives in Garden Lane, Bradford, infamously the street where 'Yorkshire Ripper' Peter Sutcliffe lived. Dick Williamson, former Sports Editor of Bradford-based *Yorkshire Sports,* was also a resident of that street. Two journalists living a matter of yards from the most wanted man in Yorkshire's history and the biggest story for many a year! Barry tells me he did benefit from the situation by hiring out his home telephone to the throng of journalists who descended on Garden Lane after Sutcliffe was arrested.

Richard Coomber is now my long-suffering business partner at Gosnay's and he too trod the well worn path to our door from the *Telegraph & Argus*. As well as being a talented journalist and author, Richard is a dead-ringer for Ken Bates in appearance, though sadly not in wealth!

Freelancing has its advantages, of course—like working your own hours and being your own boss—but like any self employed person, you only get out of the business what you are prepared to put in. Saturday nights are as anti-social as you can get, especially during the summer when our agency covers six local cricket leagues, with results and match details keeping the phone lines buzzing. We are rarely finished before 11pm on those Saturdays and the busiest part of the year is when football, rugby and cricket overlap. Few members of the modern generation are prepared to forego their Saturday nights to that extent and it's understandable—so the old timers keep making a living! Hopefully, there will long be a market for Gosnay's services but, like so many aspects of modern life, nothing stays the same for long and we are constantly looking for new outlets for the words that must have already stretched several times around the moon and back.

I had never really thought about the public perception of a freelance sports journalist before the spring of 2007. To cover a match between Leeds United and Burnley I had taken up my usual position in the Elland Road press seats—mine is at the end of a row, so I am as near to supporters as it is possible to be without actually sitting among them. I had noticed one guy who seemed fascinated by the row of lap-tops and journalists as we waited for the match to start. If I wasn't mistaken, this gentleman, who I estimated was the wrong side of 50, was a trifle star-struck as he tentatively approached the press seats.

As I was in closer proximity to him than anyone else, he approached me and politely asked what paper I was from. I could have told him any one of three publications I was working for that day, including the high circulation *News of the World*, but instead I just said I was freelance. The beam on his face disappeared in a trice. He was singularly unimpressed and shuffled his way back to his seat without another word. I wonder what his reaction would have been if I'd told him I was from *The Times*. Would he have stood there in awe and asked a hundred questions? Okay, my pride had taken a minor knock, but on reflection I had come out of it rather well because I didn't have to spend an eternity discussing my views on football, the press and any other subjects the inquisitive spectator fancied. Sometimes it's best to remain anonymous, as I've often thought when spotting TV stars being pestered for autographs in restaurants and elsewhere. Being on the staff of a paper somehow seems to carry more clout than being a freelance, yet some of the biggest names in the media are self-employed because it enables them to work for many different organisations.

Because of my Leeds United connections supporters' clubs and such regularly asked me to give talks, attend dinners and hand over trophies at local football prize-giving ceremonies. I always found the latter embarrassing because I regarded myself as a small fish in a not-too-large pond. Yet, because my name appeared nightly on the *Telegraph & Argus*'s sports pages, I was somehow afforded local celebrity status—hence the embarrassment, as I am utterly convinced most of those present at such gatherings had never heard of me. Even those who had were probably as unimpressed as the woman who came up to me at a supporters' club dinner and announced: 'Oh Mr Wray, I thought you would be much younger!'

Then there was the annual prize-giving ceremony organised by the Bradford branch of the Leeds United Supporters' Club and held at a working men's club. Bingo and that night's variety act seemed more popular than the visiting Leeds United players, even though those players were household names. So I knew I had no chance. I'd been quite critical of Don Revie's team around that time, so when my name on the guest list was read out after Billy Bremner's, I received the kind of boos normally reserved for a drag act at the Glasgow Empire. I took it all in good spirit and at least it meant my opinions had sparked some reaction among the *Telegraph & Argus*'s readers. Being booed to the rafters was better than silence, or so I told myself.

Yes, people's perceptions of journalists can be unkind, and I am convinced their views are to some extent framed by how TV dramas portray journalists. Why is it that script-writers repeatedly paint newspaper journalists as badly dressed, hard-nosed untrustworthy cretins who would shop their own mothers to get a story? Yes, you'll find some rotten apples in every orchard, but don't write off the whole crop as bad.

When asked what I did for a living, I used to tell people proudly that I was a sports journalist, mainly covering Leeds United. Unless they were totally disinterested in football, most of them thought I had the best job in the world and said so. Since Leeds' spectacular fall from grace, the job doesn't carry quite the same glamour.

There was a moment, while arriving for a holiday with Helen in Tunisia, when we both wished my documents had contained the words 'office worker' as a job description. As we were filing through passport control, a uniformed official seemed to be taking much longer over my passport than anyone else's. It was obvious that he didn't realise I was a sports journalist and thought I was entering his country to write dreadful things about the Tunisian way of life. As I was ushered away, Helen was more than a little alarmed, especially as she was prevented from immediately following me to the room where my luggage was meticulously searched and I was interrogated over my reasons for visiting the country.

When she was finally told she could join me, Helen told everyone within earshot that if we were never seen again they should report it to the proper authorities. A trifle over the top, I thought, but better safe than sorry!

16

SIR ALEX, GEORGE GRAHAM AND THE ROTTWEILER

When Esther Rantzen fronted the TV programme *That's Life* **she exposed a Jobs-worth of the Week. Good for her.** If Esther's researchers had scoured the country's football grounds they would have found candidates galore for the accolade. What is it that comes over those perfectly normal people who somehow undergo a metamorphosis as soon as they don a uniform? Mild-mannered librarians and factory workers suddenly become prime candidates for the part of Dracula.

They patrol car parks and entrances to the inner sanctums of stadiums with all the aggression of fire-breathing dragons. They may have seen you show a season press ticket time after time but if you've mislaid your pass they take immense pleasure in adopting a 'you shall not pass' mentality. There are exceptions, of course, and helpful security men can be a pressman's best friend. Yet many seem to undergo a common sense by-pass—and the more braid they wear, the dimmer they seem to become!

Clubs issue season press passes to those journalists who regularly attend home games but when you visit an away ground you have to apply to the club in advance for a press pass for that match only. In the days before fax machines and e-mails, you had to hope Her Majesty's Royal Mail had done its job so your pass would be waiting for you to collect on match-day. It was always a big relief when an envelope was produced at the ticket office with your name and newspaper written on it.

It wasn't unknown for members of the public to attempt to collect pressmen's passes under false pretences, so many clubs now insist on proof of identity before handing passes over. Of course there were times when clubs claimed they hadn't received a press ticket application, even though you had taken the precaution of using a first class stamp. In such circumstances, proof of identity and the newspaper's letterhead usually did the trick.

Yet I vividly recall an occasion when my heart sank and I thought I would be locked out of Highbury, Arsenal's then home, for a game against Leeds United. The commissionaire guarding the press entrance was supposed to have the envelopes containing all the allotted press tickets for the game. Unfortunately, after sifting meticulously through every envelope twice, he couldn't find one bearing my name and newspaper. Similarly, there was no pass for Don Warters, who was then working for the *Yorkshire Evening Post*. We had both travelled with the team and insisted we had applied for passes and booked telephones in the press box, so we could file our match reports to our respective newspapers. That carried no weight whatsoever with the little Hitler who insisted it was more than his job was worth to let us through. Nor would he take any notice of several London-based pressmen who knew us and vouched for us.

At that moment Don Revie appeared on the scene and, although he had enough on his plate preparing his team for an important match, the Leeds manager pleaded our case and vouched for our bona fide credentials. Only then did the commissionaire back down and let us through. We were in good time to file the two teams to our offices as if nothing had happened.

In all my years of sports writing I have been late for a match only once. Leeds United were playing at Birmingham's St Andrews ground and I had lost my way somewhere between the motorway and the stadium. Then, when I finally discovered somewhere to park the car, I faced a long walk, having found myself on the wrong side of the ground. By the time I took my place in the press box the game was 20 minutes old. Fortunately, one of my colleagues, who had made his own way to the stadium and arrived on time, took my call from the office and kindly sent over the teams and the first 150 words of the match report before I turned up somewhat breathless. I still try to arrive at Elland Road at least an hour and a half before the start, even though traffic congestion is nowhere near as bad since Leeds fell down the divisions.

For some years Leeds employed an ex fireman to guard the entrance to their training ground at Thorp Arch, near Wetherby. Jack Williamson was dubbed The Rottweiler by visitors who dared to attempt entry with or without the appropriate pass. Jack took his job so seriously that when foreign dignitaries arrived he would greet them in their own language by welcoming them on behalf of Leeds United Football Club, the chairman and the board of directors!

He would keep prompt-cards, bearing the greeting in countless languages, in his pocket and produce them with great pride when needed. Woe-betide anyone who tried to trick his or her way past Jack. I always got on well with him and had no cause for complaint whatsoever, though there was an hilarious occasion when Jack tried to prevent my wife Helen from entering the training ground in case she passed on Leeds' tactical secrets to Sir Alex Ferguson!

Leeds were due to play Manchester United the next day but Helen wouldn't know a volley from a back-pass and at that time I doubt whether she even knew who Sir Alex was. If someone had persuaded her to phone up the Manchester

United supremo and, by some miracle, her call had been put through, the brief conversation would have gone something like this: Helen: 'Good morning, is that Sir what's his name? I thought I would tell you what lovely white shirts and shorts Leeds United will be wearing when they come to play your team tomorrow. I've just been to the training ground and I saw the players running around to keep warm. Someone had kindly given them some gloves to wear because it was very cold. The players were kicking a football. Sometimes it went into a net and sometimes it went high over the goals into someone's garden. I bet the owner of the house wasn't very pleased. His lovely flowers must have been ruined. Anyway I must end this call because my John is waiting for me after interviewing George Graham and I can't waste good shopping time. Nice to speak to you, Sir Alec, isn't it? Goodbye.'

I had called in at Thorp Arch to see George, who was then the Leeds manager, as I needed to write a preview of the game. Helen decided to accompany me as there is a shopping complex near the training ground and I promised to take her there after the interview. Now George always was a lady's man and when he spotted Helen he ignored Jack's protests and politely invited her on to the training pitch, insisting I introduce her. George was a charming host, I got my interview and everyone was happy, except perhaps The Rottweiler, who returned to his 'kennel'—a hut at the training ground entrance—with his tail between his legs, defeated on this occasion but eager to fight another day.

Possibly Jack's most embarrassing moment came when the players decided he should be thrown into a large pond a few yards from his hut. He emerged, dripping wet and furious, especially as his treasured mobile phone sank without trace. The hut has long since gone, but in common with most professional clubs, Leeds have a security barrier at the training ground entrance and an intercom which connects visitors to a telephone in reception.

Another amusing incident occurred at Huddersfield Town where *Yorkshire Post* football writer Barry Foster, a thoroughly good friend but not renowned for his modesty, arrived at the press entrance without his season pass, which he had left in his parked car some distance away. Barry is normally meticulous in his preparations for everything from a football match to a holiday to some far flung outpost. The commissionaire insisted on the pass being shown, much to Barry's disgust, especially as he was a regular visitor to the ground and his picture often accompanied his match reports. Presumably the commissionaire wasn't a Yorkshire Post reader. Barry stared at the guy barring his way, pointed in his own direction and said in a sarcastic tone: 'Just look at the face. Don't you know who I am?'

Unfortunately he didn't—and Barry never forgot his pass again. Barry has that wonderful quality of being able to laugh at himself and we've had many a chuckle over that incident at Huddersfield over the years.

Other people's misfortunes have a habit of causing amusement, especially when the victims are—how can I put this—cautious with their money. Denis Lowe was for many years the *Daily Telegraph's* respected chief northern football writer and a correspondent for the BBC. Denis looked after every penny and was rarely seen at the front of the queue when rounds of drinks were being ordered. So the poor man received little sympathy when, after one of many excursions into Europe, he arrived back at Leeds-Bradford Airport so weighed down with duty-free drinks that the carrier bags burst, spilling their contents on to the tarmac. The liquor flowed in all directions and passengers needed great care to avoid stepping on broken glass. Rarely have I seen a pressman so close to tears.

If Denis was at the back of the queue at the bar when drinks were being paid for, he was usually at the front when free food was being served in the press rooms of football grounds all over the north. A big man who readily owned up to his passion for free grub, he would doubtless have appreciated a remark made at his funeral tea: 'At least the sandwiches are safe today.'

Accompanying footballers on trips to matches can be a hazardous business, as the *Yorkshire Evening Post*'s Phil Brown discovered on a journey into Eastern Europe with Leeds before the Berlin Wall came down. The team coach had just pulled up at 'Checkpoint Charlie' when two very surly border guards climbed aboard the coach to do a spot-check. Quick as a flash, Jack Charlton pointed at the ageing reporter and managed to keep a straight face as he bawled: 'Here he is, guys. This is the man you want.'

Phil immediately went a whiter shade of pale as he envisaged being thrown into jail behind the Iron Curtain on suspicion of being a spy. Fortunately, the guards either didn't understand Big Jack's broad North East accent or they saw the joke. Either way, a very relieved Phil was allowed to complete his journey once a full check of the coach and its contents had been made. There is no doubt that Jack and the rest of the team would have sprung to Phil's rescue if those guards had turned nasty, but they all enjoyed a good laugh at the reporter's expense.

When Leeds United were in their pomp they had a police outrider to guide the team bus through congested traffic from their hotel to the ground they were visiting. Yet on one occasion the outrider failed to arrive and Don Revie, who was a stickler for punctuality, feared the team would arrive late. In those days the BBC carried immense respect and Don had appeared so many times on that channel that he almost felt part of the organisation. So, with the team bus caught in a particularly long jam, he opened the coach door, ordered the driver to overtake the queue and bellowed 'BBC' at anyone questioning the bus's right to jump the queue!

Don was wise enough to know that shouting 'Leeds

United' at the motorists he was passing in opposition territory would have risked the staging of a deliberate road block by rival supporters. As it was, they waved him through before realising who was doing the shouting or the identity of the other men on board the coach. I doubt very much that a football manager would get away with that tactic nowadays but it certainly worked for Don who got his team to the game on time, avoiding the hefty fine that would have been imposed for a late arrival.

David Harvey, the Leeds and Scotland goalkeeper, was a fellow Horsforth resident for a time so, as my car was being repaired, he offered to give me a lift home when the team coach arrived back in the club car park from an away trip. David, who was nicknamed Suave by his team-mates because he was rarely to be found smartly dressed, enjoyed nothing better than going into the countryside to shoot rabbits. We had been away for a couple of days and, as I climbed into the front passenger seat of his vehicle, my nostrils were attacked by an offensive smell. Glancing over my shoulder I saw a pile of rabbits which David had presumably shot earlier in the week! I never did find out whether he ate those rabbits but I was pleased he didn't offer me one.

17

MANAGERIAL
MERRY-GO-ROUND

Discounting caretaker-bosses, Leeds United have had 16 managers since I started covering the club in Don Revie's era. In order, they have been Revie, Brian Clough, Jimmy Armfield, Jock Stein, Jimmy Adamson, Allan Clarke, Eddie Gray (twice), Billy Bremner, Howard Wilkinson, George Graham, David O'Leary, Terry Venables, Peter Reid, Kevin Blackwell, Dennis Wise and Gary McAllister.

Their characters and abilities varied enormously and their spells in charge ranged from 44 days (Clough) to 13 years (Revie). I have to admit that after putting countless questions to those 16 managers, there are few answers I haven't heard and, when attending press conferences these days, I am usually able to predict the answers. You get to know how managers think. Without exception they are cautious individuals who, no matter how they feel in private, **never** describe their team's next opponents as easy. That would be inviting extra criticism should their team lose and, if a school for managers existed, playing up the quality of the opposition to the press would be among the early lessons taught.

When I started out, press conferences were rare—usually reserved for the appointment or firing of managers—but now clubs are obliged to hold pre- and post-match conferences, usually attended by the manager. Sadly, there is a tendency for managers occasionally to send their assistants to face the press. Despite the interesting things he often had to say before his departure to Tottenham, Gus Poyet, Dennis Wise's then right hand man, brought a frown to the faces of radio interviewers as listeners found the Uruguayan's accent almost impossible to understand.

They've had all kinds of accents at Elland Road over the years—from South American and Australian to Norwegian and Swedish—but Poyet's was undoubtedly the most difficult to fathom over the air waves. When he first arrived at Leeds United from his native Scotland in his teens, Eddie Gray was barely decipherable to English listeners when interviewed, yet he became an accomplished BBC Radio Leeds summariser, as easy to understand as any Englishman. Despite spending so many years living in a village near Harrogate, Eddie still trots out a few Glaswegian phrases from time to time, but I never need to ask him to repeat himself during conversations.

Journalists want managers to be flamboyant characters, ever ready with a printable quote. Don Revie wasn't the most charismatic of managers but he, possibly more than any of his successors in the job, appreciated the value of publicity and went out of his way to ensure Leeds United were always in the headlines. He never minded being telephoned at home, was always available to local pressmen before training sessions and treated us as part of the Leeds United family. As I've already mentioned, many of the southern-based press didn't like him and were probably envious of his success. He publicly crossed swords with some of his fiercest critics who usually came off worst.

Revie had an aura of authority about him. He was a big man who commanded immense respect among his players and staff. I am reliably told that when players dared to knock on his door in search of a rise in pay, they did so in fear and trepidation. Yet to a man they described him as a father figure who protected them like sons and in return he commanded unstinting loyalty. His superstitions were legendary and journalists loved to recount his habit of wearing the same lucky blue suit for years, his refusal to return through the door of his home in the morning if he had left something behind, and his encouragement when players insisted on going through countless 'lucky' rituals during the build-up to kick-off time. When Don set off for work one morning and left his briefcase behind he insisted on his wife Elsie passing it to him so he wouldn't have to go back inside.

Then there was the tale of the gipsy who was called into Elland Road by Don to remove a curse from the ground after a series of bad results. Thankfully I wasn't a witness to the proceedings, but I am reliably informed that the ritual involved the gipsy urinating on all four corners of the pitch!

A couple of days before Leeds' ill-fated FA Cup Final defeat against Second Division Sunderland, I deigned to remind Don that his team hadn't lost in over 21 hours' FA Cup football. He grimaced and replied: 'Never tell me things like that. These records must end some time.' Then he wrapped his huge hands round a table leg and breathed a sigh of relief. 'It's all right now,' he grinned. 'I've touched wood.'

Soon after his appointment as manager in 1961, Revie almost took Leeds into the old third division, but they survived. Under his guidance Leeds won the League Cup, FA Cup, Second Division Championship, First Division Championship, European Fairs Cup and UEFA Cup, as well as being cheated out of the European Cup Winners' Cup by a referee who was subsequently banned for his handling of the final. Don was Manager of the Year three times and became Manager of England in July, 1974, after 13 years in charge at Leeds and six days before his 48th birthday. He succeeded World Cup winner Sir Alf Ramsey, though Joe Mercer had a short spell as caretaker-manager in between.

Like all England managers, Don had his share of run-ins with the press during his three years in the job and was never able to repeat the success he had enjoyed as a club manager.

Nor was his relationship with the scribes improved when he quit the England post in controversial circumstances to become the highly paid soccer supremo to the United Arab Emirates, accepting a contract reportedly worth £340,000, tax-free, over four years. He was subsequently charged with bringing the game into disrepute over the manner of his departure from the England job and banned from taking any job in English football for 10 years, though the ban was lifted on appeal. During his spell in charge, England won 14 games, lost seven and drew eight.

Sir Alf's record, in contrast, was 16 defeats in 113 matches. Don was sacked from his job in the Emirates in the summer of 1980, receiving a reported £90,000 in compensation. He then managed Emirates club side Al Nasr, quitting in 1984 because Elsie couldn't settle in Cairo.

In May, 1988, he cut a sad figure as he returned to Elland Road in a wheelchair, struck by the debilitating motor neurone disease which eventually killed him. More than 7,000 fans turned out to pay tribute to the man who had brought so much glory to the city of Leeds and its football club. Under the made-up by-line of John Parry I wrote in the *Daily Express*:

> On a tide of emotion, Revie was wheel-chaired into the Elland Road stadium where for 13 years he ruled supreme.
>
> Kevin Keegan and a host of glittering stars from past and present turned out to pay homage to the Don…His doting subjects on the terraces wallowed in nostalgia as Bremner, Charlton, Clarke and Co, members of the 'Super-Leeds' team, returned to form a guard of honour. On the pitch, Paul Gascoigne treated Rangers boss Graeme Souness to a close-up view of his £2million rated talent. The unsettled Newcastle marksman teamed up with Souness in an All-Star

Eleven beaten by Leeds.

If Gascoigne fancies joining the exodus of English stars across the border he gave Souness the nudge by beating England keeper Peter Shilton with the game just five minutes old. But Leeds made Revie's night by roaring back with goals by Ian Baird and John Sheridan.

Even the customary non appearance of George Best could not spoil Revie's special occasion, with receipts from a 7,305 crowd shared by motor neurone patients and Leeds City Council's 'Give For Life' campaign.

Don died a year later and fittingly his ashes were scattered at Elland Road in a private ceremony attended by his family. Leeds named their all-seater Kop after him and his name will always be synonymous with the club.

When he left Leeds, Don recommended midfielder Johnny Giles as his successor but, after originally seeming to go along with their former manager's wishes, the directors rejected the advice and went for Brian Clough instead. When it seemed Giles would be the man to take over, I drove to Johnny's house in the leafy Leeds suburb of Weetwood, accompanied by Don Warters, from the *Yorkshire Evening Post*.

Johnny gave us an in-depth interview about his plans for the club's future and how he would approach the job. He asked us to check with him the next morning that he had, indeed, got the job before we could use the story. Our articles never appeared! The rumour was that, in the meantime, Billy Bremner had applied for the job and the directors didn't want to upset Billy by appointing Johnny. So chairman Manny Cussins and his board turned to Brian Clough who left Brighton to take over at Leeds on a four year contract which he never signed.

I've already described my tempestuous relationship with Clough and the way the club was tearing itself apart during his 44 days in charge. So on to Jimmy Armfield, the absolute antithesis of Clough. Church-going Jimmy is one of the nicest men I've met in football but, in common with my wife Helen, he has great difficulty in making decisions. In Helen's case it is usually what colour she should choose for a Christmas table setting. For Jimmy, at least during his spell in charge at Leeds, it was everything from which player to leave out of the 1975 European Cup Final in Paris to whether he should have his eggs poached or boiled.

On the journey to one match, pipe-smoking Jimmy came to the back of the team coach and announced his line-up to the press. Before we reached the ground he had changed his mind. Yet I just had to like and admire him. He had played over 600 games for Blackpool as their overlapping right back and played 43 times for England, rising to captain his country. True, the team he took to the European Cup Final had been assembled by Revie, but in my view Jimmy did a good job. Revie had shied away from rebuilding the team—a task that fell to Armfield whose side never finished outside the First Division's top 10 before he was sacked in July, 1978. Jimmy, of whom it was said his indecision was final, went into journalism and broadcasting before joining the Football Association and head-hunting Terry Venables for the England post.

After Armfield, Leeds once again went for a big name and they came no bigger than Scotland legend Jock Stein. Unfortunately, Jock stayed just one day longer than Clough, becoming Scotland's manager on October 5, 1978, his 56th birthday. It was said his wife Jean was not prepared to leave Scotland for Yorkshire. Had she been more inclined to move south I am convinced Jock would have remained in the Leeds job and been as successful in England as he had been north of the border where he led Celtic to nine consecutive league crowns. He took Scotland to two World Cup finals and in his day was rated Britain's best ever club manager.

He struck me as a warm character who knew football and

footballers inside out. I found him good with the local media—not surprising as he was a close friend of Revie's—but his hurried departure left Leeds once more in the lurch. Chairman Manny Cussins said at the time: 'I am heartbroken. I suggested Mrs Stein should keep the house in Glasgow for six months or so, until we found her and Jock a home in Yorkshire, but I think that would have been unacceptable. Nothing in my lifetime has worried me more than this—not even the Brian Clough affair.'

In stepped Jimmy Adamson, the no-nonsense, straight-talking former Sunderland manager. Despite a 4–0 win against Derby at Elland Road in his first game in charge, followed by the club's first point at Liverpool for six years, a League Cup semi-final appearance and fifth place in his first season in charge, Adamson's relationship with Leeds fans quickly deteriorated. Supporters were far from impressed with some of his signings who included Wayne Entwistle, Jeff Chandler, Tony Arins and Marshall Burke. Adamson also recruited Kevin 'Jasper' Hird, Alan Curtis, John Lukic, Brian Greenhoff, Derek Parlane and Alex Sabella but with the side propping up the First Division, having taken just two points from five games, the 'Adamson Out' demonstrations grew progressively more violent.

After one home game, missiles were thrown at windows close to the boardroom and Adamson was indeed on his way out, resigning as Leeds manager and retiring from football altogether to concentrate on his passion for crown green bowls.

Having tried 'outsiders', the Leeds directors turned to prominent members of Don Revie's 'Super Leeds' team for their next three managers—Allan Clarke, Eddie Gray and Billy Bremner. I had got on well with all three in their playing days so I was delighted when they received their chance to revive the club. Unfortunately they were unable to bring back the kind of success they had enjoyed as players at the top of their profession, though Bremner took them to the promotion play-offs and the FA Cup semi-final in 1987.

First, though, it was Clarke's turn and the former goal-poacher who had never been short of confidence, arrived from Barnsley where he had guided them to promotion from the Fourth Division at the first attempt and taken them to a high placing in Division Three. His deputy, Martin Wilkinson, accompanied him, along with first team coach Barry Murphy. Allan forked out a fortune on taking Peter Barnes and Kenny Burns to the club but results failed to reflect the cash invested and he was sacked in June, 1982, with 27 months of his contract to run, having failed to save the club from relegation after their 18 years in the top flight. It was said at the time that the interest payments on the cash borrowed to pay for Barnes and Burns subsequently caused the club to sell their Elland Road ground to Leeds City Council.

It is a measure of how close to Allan I had become that I travelled with him on the saddest journey of his sporting life—to Stoke and into the Second Division. Stoke needed only a draw against West Brom to ensure their own safety and plunge Leeds down, so we travelled in Allan's car to see the club's fate decided. Clarke, ashen-faced, sat helplessly in the stand as Stoke powered their way to three goals which must have felt like daggers through the heart of the young Leeds manager who had promised supporters a trophy within three years of his appointment.

As we sped home, leaving ecstatic Stoke fans dancing in the streets, Allan told me defiantly: 'I will sweat blood to get Leeds United back in the First Division at the first attempt and I'll make sure my players sweat blood too. I wish they could have been in that stand suffering with me. It was the worst 90 minutes of my career as a manager. West Brom had nothing to play for but we can't blame them for our predicament.'

Pulling away from the terraced houses and kilns of the

Potteries, Clarke was already planning for the future. 'It is now up to everyone at the club to pull the same way and follow Norwich City's example by regaining First Division status at the first attempt,' he said. 'There is no divine right to a place in the top sphere. I will be looking for hard graft from everyone—from the directors through to the ladies who do the laundry.

'I have no money to spend but I am determined to improve the team by bringing in new blood for next season. When you are at rock bottom you become a better person and hopefully I will become a better manager.' He was sacked a month later.

When Eddie Gray succeeded Clarke, on July 4, 1982, to become Leeds' seventh manager in eight years, he had already played 539 games for the club and was appointed player-manager, though he eventually finished his playing career at the end of season 1983–84. There have been few, if any, more popular Leeds United personalities than Eddie who, like Jimmy Armfield, would have to travel many a mile to find an enemy. His first job was to call a dressing room amnesty, as he was regarded by the board as a peace-maker following alleged unrest among some of the players during Clarke's last season in charge. 'Everyone will start from scratch under my management,' he told me.

Some claimed Eddie was too nice to be a successful manager but it wasn't his affable personality that denied him the results Leeds needed to climb back into the top division. There was little cash to spend and when he was sacked on October 11, 1985, United were 14th in Division Two.

18

BREMNER AND WILKO

The statue of Billy Bremner outside Elland Road is a lasting monument to a true Leeds United legend who was in my view the greatest captain and midfield player of his generation and a joy to know.

Billy's forthright opinions were always expressed with the same passion he showed on the pitch and when he spoke, everyone listened. His was the loudest voice by far on the team coach and to sit in on one of his card schools was an education in itself. You certainly learned a few new expletives if you played the wrong card or the wee man was losing his cash. Those card sessions were played out with all the pent-up emotion of an FA Cup Final because no matter whether he was kicking a football or playing bingo, Billy always played to win.

Despite his considerable achievements as a player, Bremner was no big time Charlie. Yes, he was on speaking terms with a host of top names in the entertainment world, but the wee man from Stirling loved the company of ordinary down-to-earth folk. A chain smoker with nicotine-stained fingers, 'Chalky' as he was known by his team-mates, for his otherwise drip-white skin, struck me as a bag of nerves despite his inexhaustible ability. He had a twitch which occasionally sent his head rocking to one side and his poor time-keeping was almost as legendary as those tackles that would make a hardened criminal wince.

He gave his all for the Leeds United cause and when the time came for him to fill the manager's chair, once again he put every ounce of effort into the job. Like Eddie Gray before him, Billy didn't have a stash of cash to spend, particularly during his early days in charge. I vividly remember him phoning me at the *Telegraph & Argus* soon after his appointment and he sounded as excited as ever. 'I've just signed Cassy from Donny,' he blurted out in his strong Scottish accent. I hadn't a clue what he meant until he explained that the man he had signed was defender Brian Caswell from Doncaster Rovers where Billy had been the manager for seven years. I must admit I had never heard of Caswell and I doubt whether many Leeds fans had either. David Harle and John Buckley followed the same route from Doncaster to Leeds and the fear was that Billy was going down the same route as Jimmy Adamson by signing players who were not up to the standard the club's supporters demanded.

Eventually, he paid six-figure sums for Keith Edwards, Micky Adams, Mark Aizlewood, Glynn Snodin, Gary Williams, Bobby Davison, Vince Hilaire and Andy Williams, while future England international David Batty began his first team career under Bremner's management. Bremner was like an encouraging father to Batty, just as Don Revie had been to Billy all those years before. United finished 14th in the Second Division after Billy's first season in charge and one of his biggest mistakes was to release Denis Irwin on a free transfer. Irwin joined Oldham before enjoying a long career with Manchester United and the Republic of Ireland.

In Billy's second season, United finished fourth, missed out on promotion in the play-off final against Charlton and were denied an FA Cup Final appearance when Coventry beat them in extra time of a sparkling semi-final at Hillsborough. In the following season United finished seventh and after starting the next campaign with just six points from six matches, Billy was shown the door with 21 months of his contract to run.

The irony was that the sacking came the day after a League Cup victory at Peterborough, but the decision to part with Bremner had been made the previous weekend, after a home defeat by Chelsea. History therefore repeated itself as Bremner's predecessor Eddie Gray had been sacked after a League Cup win at Walsall in 1985.

The writing had been on the wall for some time and after a home defeat at the hands of Yorkshire neighbours Barnsley it gave me no pleasure to report in the *News of the World* that angry Leeds fans wanted Billy booted out of his job. Some fans burst through Elland Road's main entrance to stage a demo outside the boardroom, calling for their former hero's head. One fan bawled at the startled directors: 'Put down your gin and tonics and do something!'

Chairman Leslie Silver told me after the eventual sacking: 'Billy Bremner did his best and his commitment to the club was total, but we had to judge the situation on results. The pattern set in the first couple of months of any season tends to be continued unless fundamental changes are made. We have had a lot of players through the club over the last few years without the desired effect on results.'

I was sorry to see Billy become the seventh managerial casualty since Revie's departure 14 years earlier and, after returning to his old club Doncaster, he worked as a broadcaster and after-dinner speaker. I was on a day-off, wandering round Lincoln's Christmas market, when the sad news came through that Billy had died of a heart attack in Doncaster Royal Infirmary on December 7, 1997, two days short of his 55th birthday. I was among those shoe-horned into St Mary's Church, Ellington, near Doncaster, for the funeral service on December 11, attended by many of his former Leeds United colleagues. Also among the big names in the congregation were Sir Alex Ferguson, Nobby Stiles and

Dave Mackay. Many of those who turned up to pay their last respects had to be content with a place outside the church and the sheer numbers provided a fitting tribute. The club commissioned a statue of Billy which, as I mentioned at the start of this chapter, stands outside Elland Road and is a focal point for fans to gather on match days and other occasions.

Howard Wilkinson, Bremner's successor, did what Clarke, Gray and Billy all failed to do. He brought some long-awaited silverware to the club. Howard and Billy were complete opposites. Quietly spoken and studious, Howard had been a schoolteacher and a moderately successful footballer with Sheffield Wednesday, Brighton and Boston United. When he moved from his job in charge of Sheffield Wednesday in October, 1988, having also managed Boston United and Notts County, Wilkinson found Leeds languishing in 21st place in Division Two. Yet he took them to the Second Division Championship in 1990 and to the League Championship two years later. They also won the FA Charity Shield by defeating Liverpool 4–3 at Wembley.

Despite the acquisition of Eric Cantona, who never reached his full potential at Leeds, Wilko's most inspiring signing was Gordon Strachan who, at £300,000 from Manchester United, was one of football's all-time bargain buys. Wilkinson and Strachan proved a dream combination— 'Sgt Wilko', the master tactician organising the troops, and Strachan enjoying a new lease of life on the field in the later years of his career under Wilko's command.

Vinnie Jones and Lee Chapman were also crucial signings and I've written about my frustration on the day of Vinnie's arrival elsewhere in this book. I missed a phone call from the new signing but when I eventually caught up with him for a first interview I found him genuinely thrilled by the challenge he faced at Leeds United. Chairman at the time, Bill Fotherby, must have been peering into a crystal ball when he told me: 'Vinnie is the key to unlock the door to Division One for us. He will be an instant hero with the fans. I think Vinnie will give us something we haven't had since the playing days of Billy Bremner and Norman Hunter. He is a winner who cannot bear to lose. That's the spirit Bremner and Hunter always showed and there are very few players of their sort around these days.'

The fear was that Jones, not exactly noted for tip-toeing through the tulips, would ruin the club's disciplinary record which Wilkinson had worked so hard to improve. Yet Vinnie largely stayed clear of trouble during his time at Leeds and said: 'I don't go out to hurt people. I seem to be a marked man. I'm not as black as I'm painted and this move gives me a chance to make a new start and prove people wrong. It's a great move for me and Leeds are as ambitious for success as I am.'

I wrote at the time:

The public image of Vinnie Jones falls somewhere between the Boston Strangler and Attila the Hun. But the former hod carrier, who delighted in the nickname Psycho at his previous club Wimbledon, wallows in the tranquillity of countryside pursuits when he's away from the heat of soccer action.

Leeds United's £650,000 signing has been in trouble with soccer's disciplinarians more often than he cares to remember, yet he likes nothing better than escaping to the rolling acres of the Hertfordshire countryside near his home in Hemel Hempstead.

Vinnie was single at the time and he told me: 'The two passions in my life, apart from football, are shooting and fishing. I get lots of time to get away from it all, roaming the countryside fishing for trout or shooting rabbits and pheasants. My idea of heaven is jumping into my Daihatsu Jeep and taking a lamp into the hedgerows and fields to chase rabbits.'

Fotherby quipped: 'If the fish jump, Vinnie will shoot them.'

There was one time when Wilko found Vinnie pointing a gun in his direction on the team coach! Vinnie had been left out of the team and he jokingly informed the manager he was about to take retribution! Vinnie had been brought up with the Crazy Gang spirit of fun and mischief at Wimbledon where Dave Bassett signed him from non-League Wealdstone. It was a spirit Wilkinson encouraged in the Leeds dressing room and Vinnie's value in that department was every bit as important as his immense contribution on the pitch. Jones and David Batty became particularly close friends, though some of their pranks were not always appreciated by their team-mates who were usually the victims.

Wilkinson may have been a more subdued character than Bremner but he was no pushover as a boss, as Welsh international and Leeds captain Mark Aizlewood found to his cost in May, 1989. Aizlewood had been a target for the boo-boys in the Leeds crowd for some time and they turned on him again after he missed an open goal against Walsall soon after the hour. His response on heading an 83rd minute winner was to leer at the fans and give them a double V-sign which was vividly captured by photographers. Howard responded by substituting the player who had no future at Leeds after that and was sold to Bradford City in the summer for £215,000.

With the likes of Batty, Jones, Strachan, Chapman, Gary Speed and Mel Sterland, Leeds won the Second Division Championship on goal difference from Sheffield United, Chapman's winning goal at Bournemouth on the final day of the 1989–90 season confirming the club's return to the top flight. Before the match, Leeds fans turned the normally sedate seaside resort into a battleground and over 100 arrests were made. I had witnessed hooliganism many times before, of course, but calls from some quarters for Leeds to be denied promotion were rightly rejected, though the club did face yet another FA inquiry. Because the press box was so small at Bournemouth, I watched the game from a bench near the touchline and had a perfect view of Chapman's winner and the ecstatic celebrations that followed. Promotion meant a huge financial boost for the club, yet when the champagne flowed in the Leeds dressing room afterwards it was drunk from plastic cups!

There was more champers two years later, of course, when Wilko's side carried off the League Championship. Vinnie was sold on to Sheffield United just a few months after the Second Division title success to make way for Gary McAllister, and another victim from that team was goalkeeper Mervyn Day following John Lukic's return from Arsenal. I recall Wilkinson telling me after the League Championship triumph that he ought to pack in, there and then, because things could only go downhill from such a massive high. He was right, too. Wilko was sacked in September, 1996, with three years of his contract to run. His departure came after a 4–0 defeat by Manchester United at Elland Road but he remained a major figure in the game, becoming the FA's Technical Director, England's caretaker-manager twice and Under 21 boss. He managed Sunderland briefly and a team in Shanghai before joining the Board at Notts County and chairing the League Managers' Association.

It has taken a long time but Howard has finally had his achievements at Elland Road recognised in tangible form in the shape of 'Howard's Way'—the Howard Wilkinson Suite in the West Stand. The club's lavish training ground and academy at Thorp Arch—envied by many Premiership clubs—was his brainchild and lasting testimony to his forward thinking. My daily phone calls to him invariably produced interesting copy for the papers and I miss all those metaphors and similes that flowed from him in a torrent.

19

WHEN GRAHAM TOLD ME HE WAS LEAVING

Howard Wilkinson's eight years in charge had brought much-needed stability to a club that hugely under-achieved through the late seventies and most of the eighties. Yet the managerial merry-go-round was to be cranked up again with seven managers in the next 10 roller-coaster years.

George Graham, the suave Scot, who had enjoyed immense success at Arsenal, only to fall on his own sword by taking a transfer bung and being banned from world football for a year, was far from popular with Leeds supporters who disliked his obsession with defensive football as well as money. In Graham's first season in charge (1996–97) Leeds scored just 28 goals—the lowest total in all four divisions and the lowest by any team that has avoided relegation from the top flight. Yet they finished 11th and conceded just 38 goals, with only Arsenal, Aston Villa and Liverpool letting in fewer. A year later, Graham's team finished fifth and qualified for the UEFA Cup. In December, 1997, Graham signed a new contract on a reported salary of £1million a year, plus bonuses, but left to become Tottenham's manager on October 1, 1998, because he wanted to be nearer his family in London.

Leeds were so keen to keep him that they offered him the role of Football Director, with more time to spend in London, but Graham had made up his mind. I had confirmation from the horse's mouth that George was leaving before the official announcement was made. I had accompanied the team to Madeira for the second leg of a UEFA Cup first round tie against Maritimo. The match didn't kick off until 9pm and, with extra time and penalties, it was 11.45pm before it ended. United had won the first leg 1–0 at Elland Road with a goal by Jimmy Floyd Hasselbaink six minutes from the end. A goal from Maritimo's Jorge Soares, just before half time in Madeira, tied the aggregate scores and when extra time failed to produce any more goals, United won 4–1 on penalties. I was covering the match for *The Guardian* and was surprised that they managed to carry a full report despite the very late finish. There had been rumours that George was about to resign and take the Tottenham job, so, as I was employed to write the Leeds United club programme, including the manager's column, I needed to know whether George would still be in charge for the next match.

Leeds were at home to Leicester City on the Saturday and George was well aware of the tight deadline I faced. He also knew it would be ridiculous if his column looked ahead to the Leicester match if he had already left. So, on the flight home, he confided in me that he was definitely going and gave his reasons in the column. I was sworn to secrecy and kept the confidence despite being asked by several of my fellow journalists if I knew what George had decided.

I liked George and always felt, as he did, that he was made a scapegoat over the bung allegations. George regretted what he did but he was convinced there were other guilty managers who got away with financial irregularities because those in charge of the game had no desire to see its image tarnished further. I warm to people who can laugh at themselves and there were a few times during George's two years at Leeds when he shared jokes with the press against himself, just as the veteran comedian Ken Dodd has done with his audiences in the years after his investigation by the Inland Revenue.

Mind you, it wasn't all sweetness and light during Graham's two years at the helm. In fact Tony Yeboah, the Ghanaian striker who scored some spectacular goals for the Whites, provided the press with a tasty story when, on being substituted in a home game against Spurs, he angrily threw his shirt at Graham and never played for the club again. Ian Rush had been signed by Howard Wilkinson shortly before Graham's arrival and clearly the Liverpool and Wales legend's best years were behind him. Rush complained that Graham was playing him out of position on the right flank and, after being left out at the start of the 1997–98 season, Ian was shipped out to Newcastle on a free transfer.

George provided us with another good story when Leeds played his old club Arsenal at Highbury in January, 1998. Arsenal's manager, Arsene Wenger, complained about the treatment Dennis Bergkamp received from the Leeds players. George accused Wenger of whingeing and added that foreign coaches and players must learn to accept the physical and mental challenges of the English game. David O'Leary, who was to become Graham's successor later that year, had rowed with Arsenal's Patrick Vieira in the players' tunnel during the interval.

United were in the headlines for unusual reasons again in March, 1998, when the right engine of a BAe 748 turbo-prop plane taking them home from a 3–0 defeat at West Ham caught fire on take-off at Stansted. It was a frightening episode for all concerned but the pilot, Capt. John Hackett, successfully landed the plane, which ran out of runway and landed in soft ground. There were no injuries and the relieved players and staff were so grateful that they invited Capt. Hackett and his crew to be guests of honour at a home match against Chelsea, presenting them with Gucci watches as a special thank you. Capt. Hackett also received a goalkeeper's shirt with his name and the No. 1 on the back.

Until the incident at Stansted, some of Leeds United's

least sensitive supporters had used their hatred of Manchester United to justify singing a song about the Munich air crash of 1958 in which 23 passengers were killed, including eight Manchester United players. Chairman Peter Ridsdale was on Leeds' stricken plane at Stansted and in an interview I conducted with him for the club programme, Peter called for the infamous airport song to be ditched for good. He told me: 'I feel that the events at Stansted brought home to all of us the potential impact such incidents can have on football clubs and communities. I would like to think that some good can come out of our near tragedy.

'I therefore appeal to the small minority of Leeds United fans who seem to feel it is fun to have a go at Manchester United, given what happened all those years ago, to draw a line behind history, stop singing that offensive song and look forward to a rivalry that is keen but healthy and respectful. I just wonder what those people would be thinking now if the same thing had happened to us at Stansted.

'We do not want to take away the right kind of barracking of opposition fans and teams but such barracking should be kept within the bounds of decency and respectability.'

David O'Leary had been the first to open an emergency exit from the aircraft when it landed safely and when George Graham slammed the door shut on his own spell in charge of Leeds, O'Leary walked through it for his first job in management. I was pleased to see the post go to someone I had got to know during his admittedly brief and injury-hit time as a player at Leeds and his two years as Graham's assistant. O'Leary had enjoyed outstanding success as a top defender with Arsenal and the Republic of Ireland and his close association with Graham meant there was some sort of continuity.

With Ridsdale and his fellow directors sanctioning big spending, O'Leary invested heavily in top players who were so well paid that the car park at United's Thorp Arch training ground was crammed with Porsches, BMWs and even a Ferrari or two. If my Honda Civic had feelings it would definitely have suffered from an inferiority complex! I was present when the local police turned up at the manager's office one day to complain about speeding by some Leeds players in those high powered cars on the narrow country roads around Thorp Arch.

O'Leary also had to contend with the high profile court case involving Leeds players Jonathan Woodgate, Lee Bowyer and some of their friends after an Asian youth, Sarfraz Najeib, was attacked outside the Majestyk nightclub in the centre of Leeds in January, 2000. Bowyer and Woodgate continued to train and play for Leeds, though England banned them from playing for their country pending the outcome of the case. While Bowyer seemed to take it all in his stride, Woodgate looked drawn and visibly lost weight. Journalists were limited in what they could write, before and during the case, as they were bound by the law of sub-judice. The court proceedings were covered by seasoned court reporters rather than sports hacks and I can't say I was sorry about that.

Both players continued to be polite to the press, though they were understandably unwilling to do interviews with me for the club programme until the case was over. Bowyer was cleared of causing GBH with intent and affray, while Woodgate was convicted of affray and sentenced to community service. Yet the fallout from the case was to drag on and O'Leary contributed to that with his book, *Leeds United On Trial*. Ridsdale has claimed O'Leary lost the respect of the players when the book came out, and results suffered to such an extent that Leeds went into spectacular freefall.

O'Leary, who refuted his chairman's claims, had guided Leeds to their first European semi-final in 25 years but the UEFA Cup-tie against Galatasaray, in Turkey, was a tragic occasion as two Leeds fans, Kevin Speight and Chris Loftus, died of stab wounds in Istanbul the night before the first leg of the semi-final. Ridsdale, who was later to be pilloried by Leeds fans for the over-spending that took the club to the brink of oblivion, was widely praised that night in Istanbul for the way he visited the hospital where both men died and the compassion he showed. I missed the trip to Istanbul for the match but reported on most of United's games that season, saw them finish a highly respectable third and thoroughly enjoyed their Champions League adventure. Having visited Barcelona's magnificent Nou Camp to cover the 1975 European Cup semi-final, I had always wanted to report from two other renowned grounds in Europe—Real Madrid's Bernabeau and AC Milan's San Siro—and I got my wish. The facilities were superb at these two magnificent cathedrals of football, but after battling their way to the semi-final stage, O'Leary's team crashed to a 3–0 defeat in Valencia.

That Champions League semi-final took place on May 8, 2001. Just six years later, Leeds United were relegated to League One and were contemplating life in the third tier of English football for the first time in their history. Reporting on that incredible collapse has been particularly painful because you can't cover a club's fortunes for over 40 years without becoming a fan. United's hierarchy gambled heavily on qualification for the Champions League, yet they finished fourth in their Champions League season of 2000–01 and competed in the UEFA Cup for the next two years. The team finished fifth in May, 2002, but a month later O'Leary was sacked, having criticised the board over their apparent willingness to sell Rio Ferdinand, and the downward slide was on its way. O'Leary's press conferences were always well attended but one hack wore a puzzled look when he thought the manager said Leeds were going to play with a porpoise. The word the Irishman actually used, of course, was 'purpose'!

When former England manager Terry Venables arrived as O'Leary's successor, the occasion was pure showbiz. The press conference was held in a building across the road from the East Stand in Low Fields Road and everyone who was anyone in the media was there. The room's ceiling was painted black and dotted with small lights like twinkling stars. Venables breezed in, wearing a striking pink shirt, and you had to pinch yourself to remember this was the arrival of a football manager, not a Frank Sinatra comeback concert.

Before Leeds had kicked a ball in the new season, Venables suffered a massive blow with Ferdinand's sale to Manchester United for £30million, much against the manager's wishes. The sale was essential to ease the club's mounting debt but the body language between Venables and Ridsdale at the subsequent press conference told its own story. The departure of Robbie Keane to Tottenham, Olivier Dacourt to Roma, Lee Bowyer to West Ham, Jonathan Woodgate to Newcastle and Robbie Fowler to Manchester City saw more big names pass through the exit door.

The season was only two months old when I reported on Leeds fans chanting the names of O'Leary and the left-out David Batty, though Venables insisted that Batty was not match fit. There were calls for Venables' head after a 4–2 home defeat by Bolton who had started the day on the foot of the table and when Venables' side lost their fifth successive home league game it was the worst run at Elland Road in the club's history. Venables had always been a friend of the media, having spent some time as a soccer pundit on TV, and I always found him a willing and lucid communicator, but results continued to disappoint. When the fans turned on Ridsdale during Middlesbrough's second win at Leeds in 20 visits, the chairman watched the second half on TV in the directors' lounge. The axe was about to hit Venables' neck.

That game, in March, 2003, proved to be the manager's last in charge and 10 days after Venables' departure, Ridsdale resigned as the headlines just kept writing themselves. Peter Reid was rapidly placed in charge of the team, initially for the final eight games of the season. Reid rescued Leeds from relegation, with immense help from Mark Viduka who scored 11 goals in those eight matches, including a hat-trick in the 6–1 demolition of Charlton. Reid's sojourn at Elland Road was short-lived, however. Hamstrung by a shortage of cash, the Scouser still managed to retain his sense of humour and kept the local press amused with his outlook on life. Yet, faced with a paper-thin squad, he brought in a host of foreign players on loan and it just didn't work. Reid was sacked on November 10, 2003, after the team had taken just eight points from the opening 11 matches, culminating in a 6–1 trouncing at Portsmouth.

Eddie Gray was brought back and placed in temporary charge but the likeable Scot was sacked six months later after failing to keep the club in the Premiership. If Ridsdale was known as Publicity Pete for the way he courted the media, Gray's successor Kevin Blackwell was just as media friendly. His press conferences were held in his office at the training ground because the number of pressmen turning up for match previews had dwindled to half a dozen or so.

Kevin enjoyed a close relationship with the local press and the conversations would last long after the official business of the press conferences was over. Mind you, Kevin did guard his privacy when I accidentally left my voice recorder on his table. When I got it back the next day the tape had been wiped, presumably to ensure I hadn't recorded private conversations. The same thing happened a few weeks later and once again the tape was wiped. I hadn't left that voice recorder on the manager's table on purpose—honest. Kevin was genuinely proud to be Leeds United's manager and it was a huge blow to him when, after taking the club to within 90 minutes of a return to the Premiership through the Championship play-offs, he was sacked by chairman Ken

Bates with the club second from bottom after one win in eight league games. Ironically, the sacking came the day after a 3–1 Carling Cup win over Barnet—Blackwell's first club.

The parting was far from chummy as Blackwell was left to battle for compensation, having made remarks which Bates interpreted as a sleight on the way the club was being run. Although head coach John Carver was placed in temporary charge, his days were numbered after one win and four successive defeats.

20

A WISE APPOINTMENT?

From the moment Ken Bates became Leeds United's chairman, in January, 2005, it was rumoured Dennis Wise would be heading north to fill the manager's chair. The close relationship between the two started at Chelsea where Bates had sanctioned Wise's signing as a player. Bates is godfather to Wise's children and the Leeds manager was the only employee at Elland Road allowed to refer to the chairman as 'Batesy'.

Kevin Blackwell spent much of his reign looking over his shoulder, suspecting Bates was awaiting his chance to wield the axe and bring in his man Wise. Caretaker-manager John Carver suspected he, too, was merely keeping the seat warm for Wise who was doing a good job as manager of Swindon. From my point of view, I was sorry to see Blackwell and Carver go, but pleased to have a big name at Leeds who would mean something to those guys on the national newspapers who accept or reject my stories. If Dennis Wise said something, it made news. With respect, when Kevin Blackwell held court, few seemed to care on the desks of the nationals. Not that Dennis was full of trust for the northern press when he first arrived. In fact he openly admitted a year into his reign that he 'distrusted you lot'. Later he was much more comfortable with the media men he had got to know through his weekly press conferences.

The relationship between a manager and the press has to

be worked at on both sides, for in truth we need each other. Wise and Bates fell out with the *Yorkshire Evening Post* big-time—partly over the tone of some articles during Wise's first season in charge, but mainly through the publication of ultra critical letters from Leeds fans. It's not the job of a newspaper to censure the views of its readers but Wise and Bates felt the letters were given too much prominence at a time when the club needed a united front as it battled to turn round massive debts and bad results.

One story, in particular, angered the Leeds hierarchy as a local journalist telephoned the Football Association to check whether Leeds had used more than the permitted number of loan players in a match. The club felt that without that phone call the genuine oversight by Leeds would have gone unnoticed by the FA—hence the call was looked on as treachery. A radio man was picked out for a grilling from Wise for running the story, even though it turned out he was not the guy who had phoned the FA in the first place. The identity of the so-called culprit eventually came to light and for some time he was shunned by the men in charge at the club.

Not that journalists were the only victims of a witch-hunt. When Wise held his press conference after a home 2–1 win against Crystal Palace in February, 2007, he revealed that a member of his first team squad had given details of the Leeds line-up to the opposition between noon and 1pm that day and, as a consequence, would never play for Leeds United again. It was a sensational story, even by Leeds standards, and Dennis's refusal to name the guilty man left journalists to play a dangerous guessing game. Suddenly, players' agents were contacting the Press Association to deny their clients' involvement as the rumour machine gathered pace.

Shaun Derry felt particularly aggrieved when Wise failed to come out and deny to reporters that the midfielder was the 'mole'. Suspicion had fallen on Derry because he had played for Crystal Palace and therefore knew some of their players.

Yet Shaun was totally innocent. I did eventually discover the 'guilty' man's identity, though I kept it to myself. My view at the time was that Wise was wrong to raise the issue at that post-match press conference. It is commonplace for players from different clubs to telephone each other and unwittingly pass on information which may in hindsight benefit the opposition. I, and many other journalists, just felt Wise's reaction was over the top and perhaps reflected the pressure he was under to get results.

In Wise's defence, I understand he did not know the culprit's identity until some time after the so-called offence, but the relationship between the manager and Derry was damaged beyond repair. It was therefore hardly surprising that, when Leeds found themselves short of midfield players and Wise asked Derry to return early from a loan spell at Crystal Palace, the player refused. Wise then used the press to vent his anger and denounce Derry's decision.

Palace signed Derry at the end of his loan period, Leeds pocketed a fee and saved on the player's sizeable wages—and Wise was a happy man. Even if he had known the mole's identity from the outset and decided to keep it secret, Wise could hardly have kept denying names thrown at him by the press until someone eventually came up with the right name. What would the manager have done then?

Dennis never did reveal the mole's identity but at another post-match press conference he was scathing in his criticism of Kevin Nicholls for a different 'offence'. Nicholls was dropped and stripped of the captaincy after seeking a transfer back to his old club Luton—one of Leeds' rivals for Championship survival. Wise's job was difficult enough without having one of his key players looking to jump ship and when relegation was confirmed by Hull City's victory at Cardiff on April 28, 2007, United were condemned to third tier football for the first time in their history. I missed the match, as I was attending a family wedding on the Sussex coast, but I couldn't resist keeping in touch with events as they unfolded with regular calls to a colleague in the press box.

After the nightmare of relegation and administration, Leeds United emerged with that Football League imposed 15 point penalty, with some pundits tipping them to go down yet again. Yet the punishment only served to make Wise and his players even more determined to overcome what they and the fans saw as a massive injustice. There was a siege mentality about the place and every victory was immediately followed by a huddle inside the centre circle. With Wise and chief coach Gus Poyet pulling the strings off the field, those 15 points were wiped out in the shortest possible time and Wise's demeanour noticeably mellowed. No longer falling out with the press, he showed the warm side of his personality during the regular Thursday press conferences at Thorp Arch. Those sessions became progressively longer and on more than one occasion my dictaphone ran out of tape as Dennis held court. I like to think trust was earned on both sides and the information readily made available to the press by the manager certainly made our jobs easier and more enjoyable.

It still seems incongruous covering matches between Leeds United and Cheltenham, for instance, but there is a camaraderie at this level that is rarely found in the top echelons of the game where egos hold sway. Dave 'Harry' Bassett, Wise's former Wimbledon chum, was drafted in to succeed Poyet as assistant manager when the Uruguayan left to join Tottenham, and Bassett proved as media friendly as ever. Never short of a word or several thousand, Dave knows the game inside out, but soon after his arrival at Leeds, his penchant for forgetting players' names surfaced big-time. Wise delegated a post-match press conference to him and Dave managed to get three Leeds players' names wrong.

'Cheeky Chappie' Wise milked the situation for all it was worth by turning up at the next Thursday press conference with a Dennis name badge on his tracksuit 'in case Harry forgets who I am.' It turned out that when Bassett signed Wise for Wimbledon he got Dennis's name wrong for the first three months!

So it's not just the press who occasionally slip up over players' names, as Jermaine Beckford, Tresor Kandol and Jonny Howson will testify. Dave called them Darren Beckford, Trevor Kandol and James Howson! The joke was on United's then assistant boss when a listener to BBC Radio Leeds called him Mike Bassett, during a phone-in.

When Wise made a sudden departure in January, 2008, to become Newcastle United's Executive Director of Football, bizarrely based in London, Bassett and first team coach John Gannon soon followed him through the exit door and in came Gary McAllister, the club's seventh manager in less than six years. There's a saying among the press corps covering Leeds United that you can't take your eye off the ball for a second at one of the newsiest clubs in the country. There will be no blank spaces on the sports pages while ever Leeds United are in existence and Wise's hasty retreat, followed rapidly by McAllister's appointment, initially until the end of the 2007–08 season, kept the words flowing.

Whereas Wise's arrival had been greeted with mixed feelings by Leeds fans, many of whom resented his past Chelsea connections, the return to the club of former captain McAllister was universally applauded. I was as pleased as anyone to see him land the job, as I used to ghost his captain's column in the programme and enjoyed a good working relationship with the likeable Scot. Mind you, I wasn't quite sure how to take his greeting as he arrived in the Elland Road press room after his first match in charge. Shaking me by the hand he made some reference to old faces and I felt like retorting: 'Less of the old.' In retrospect, I'm sure Gary meant familiar faces—at least I hope he did!

It gave me no pleasure at all to report on an abject 2–0

defeat against Tranmere as Gary's reign got off to a losing start, but he had only begun the job three days earlier, so could hardly be held responsible. The tumultuous welcome he received when he took his place in the dugout before the game reflected the esteem in which he has been held ever since his six years as a Leeds player. Gary was a hugely influential member of the 1992 League Championship winning side under Howard Wilkinson's management, and although some Leeds supporters felt he had left Leeds to join Coventry in 1996 for the money, they soon forgave him.

There was universal sympathy for Gary when he left his job as Coventry's manager in 2004 to look after his wife Denise, who was suffering from breast cancer and subsequently lost her battle for life. Few Leeds managers have started their jobs with as much goodwill from the fans. McAllister entered the Leeds post knowing his reputation would stand or fall on future results, not memories of a distinguished playing career, and he made all the right noises at his first press conference. He is a strong disciple of entertaining football—getting the ball down and passing—while recognising the need to win the battles for possession first. I hope he enjoys as much success in his managerial career as he did as arguably the best attacking midfield player Leeds have had since he last kicked a ball for them in 1996.

Though nowhere near as controversial in his outlook as Wise, McAllister benefits from his past association with Leeds and fully understands the frustration of supporters who are craving for a return to the good times after so much turmoil and disappointment. Whether he can deliver in the long term remains to be seen, but the initial reaction from the players to his arrival was reassuringly positive and after a series of encouraging results by the side under McAllister's management in League One, the Scot was rewarded with an extended contract before the end of the season.

Assistant manager Steve Staunton and first team coach

Neil McDonald also had their contracts extended and McAllister said at the time: 'The club are giving us a fair crack. It is a show of faith in the three of us and it took me all of two seconds to say yes to the new contract. This is one of the top 10 jobs in the country even though we are in the third tier of English football at the moment. I will be moving back to live in Yorkshire and my eldest son is delighted because he was born here when I was a player at Leeds.

'There is a wee bit of continuity and the players know where they stand. They are fully aware of the direction in which we are trying to take the club. I feel results could have been better—we have had too many draws—but the chairman has seen improvements around the place. I have tried to introduce the players to a few things based on my experience of playing in the Premiership and working under some of the game's top managers. We can still take things up a few notches—I am sure there is more in the players' locker.'

Leeds' record under McAllister's stewardship, up to and including the play-offs, read 10 wins, five draws and five defeats, with 26 goals scored and 17 conceded. However, most of the players he inherited were signed by Wise and had to adapt to a different style of play under the new boss. McAllister has already been hailed for his general approach to the job and in particular for giving first team opportunities to talented local youngsters including Jonny Howson, Fabian Delph and Aidan White. Yet, like all managers, Macca will rightly be judged on results when he has assembled his own team.

21

THE CHAIRMEN

The days when football chairmen were low-profile individuals whose names were largely unknown by football supporters have long gone. Nowadays you are just as likely to read on the sports pages the forthright views of Leeds chairman Ken Bates as you are to find quotes from players and managers. Chairmen are not only the men who sign the cheques and have pride of place in the directors' box. In many cases they are personalities in their own right and I've witnessed lots of them signing autographs in club car parks and hotels. Bates is a classic case of the high profile chairman. Never a man to hide his light under a bushel, he used his programme notes while in charge at Chelsea to pass judgement on a whole range of football-related issues about which he cared passionately and he has done exactly the same since rescuing Leeds United from oblivion.

For many years, as editor of the Leeds United club programme, I ghost-wrote columns for the club's captains, managers and chairmen, but Bates insisted on writing his own programme notes. I wasn't sorry about that, especially as his views sometimes sailed so close to the legal wind that I would have advised much greater caution. Not that Ken would have taken any notice.

He fought a one-sided contest with former Leeds director Melvyn Levi through the club programme, and other adversaries have found themselves similarly slated by Bates's vitriolic pen. His programme notes are rarely less than controversial and entertaining.

During the 2007–08 season the abuse of referees in this country by managers, staff and players was topical and Bates wrote in the Leeds United programme for the match against Brighton that zero tolerance should be shown to offenders by the authorities. Sick of the 'bullying and intimidation of officials', he suggested a hard-hitting plan which the FA should try from the following season as follows:

1. Managers and staff who intimidate and/or criticise officials to have a four-week ban, during which they must not go near the training ground or stadium on match days, together with a fine of four weeks wages to be paid to the FA.

2. Punishment for players' dissent to be an automatic red card with a four-match suspension and similar fines. Players who bully and intimidate the referee when they are not involved with the incident to get two yellow cards (not a red) to be included in the totting-up process. Yellow and red cards for dissent to automatically incur a fine of one week's wage and three weeks' wages, respectively.

3. Players guilty of misbehaviour to be ineligible to represent England at any level. Foreign players to have an alternative sanction.

'Draconian? Yes. Zero tolerance should be the order of the day,' Bates wrote. 'Then we can perhaps reclaim our beautiful game. When we have demonstrated it works, perhaps the gutless Home Office will take note and apply similar measures to the streets.'

When Bates decided to take the club programme in-house, it was no reflection on how I and my colleagues at Gosnay's Sports Agency had performed our duties for so many years. It was simply that the chairman wanted to save money and give the club more control by taking everything in-house, from writing the programme and running the website to controlling the catering. As I write this book, he has taken the controversial decision to reject BBC Radio Leeds' offer for commentary coverage of Leeds United's league matches in the 2008–09 season, explaining the amount they were prepared to pay for the contract fell well short of his valuation.

When the decision was made public there was an outcry from those fans who had always felt admirably served by Radio Leeds and their commentators. Many of those commentators, including John Helm, Harry Gration, Jon Champion, Peter Drury, Bryn Law and Ian Dennis, have gone on to national TV and radio fame, yet from the moment Bates launched his digital station Yorkshire Radio it was the beginning of the end for Radio Leeds' core Leeds United coverage. Bates takes everything 'in-house', so it was obvious to me that it was only a matter of time before Yorkshire Radio had exclusive commentary rights for Leeds United's league matches.

I could see the financial reasons behind the chairman's decision to take the match-day programme in-house, though the short notice we received from the club—just a few weeks before the start of a new season—was unfortunate.

I first met Ken Bates in his office in Elland Road's East Stand, less than an hour after the press conference called to mark his arrival at the club. Also there was Neil Jeffries, editor of the official club magazine, *Leeds, Leeds, Leeds*. It was immediately apparent to both of us that the chairman wanted things done his way, which was fair enough, considering he had sunk his own money into the club. At a subsequent meeting about the programme's content he made it perfectly clear that the Supporters Club page would be ditched.

I reasoned that the Supporters Club had many thousands of members, the page was extremely popular with those members and the many names mentioned in each edition sold countless copies. It was an argument I was never going to win, especially as Bates had plans to introduce a Members Club, run by Leeds United. The Supporters Club, which had existed for many years and had branches spread around the country, was to be marginalised in favour of the new organisation. I had always enjoyed an excellent relationship with the Supporters Club's officials and it left me in a very embarrassing situation, especially as I had been a guest at the SC's Player of the Year dinner since its inception in 1971 when Norman Hunter was the first winner. I think Supporters Club officials understood there was nothing I could do to save their column and I am pleased to say I still exchange Christmas cards with their chairman, Ray Fell.

Whatever your views on Ken Bates and the way his buy-out of the club left so many creditors licking their wounds, his argument that he saved Leeds United from going under is valid. There were many publicity seekers who contacted the press claiming to have sufficient funds, but Bates was the man who put his money where his mouth was. Much of the criticism he attracted was forgotten when Leeds rapidly wiped out the 15 point deficit imposed by the Football League for the way the club entered administration in May, 2007.

Bates can reduce adversaries to trembling wrecks with a few well chosen words, but he can also be an amusing and charming companion who has made himself available to the fans at various sports forums. It was a huge blow to him when head coach Gus Poyet left for Tottenham and manager Dennis Wise later quit to become part of Kevin Keegan's new regime at Newcastle, but the chairman made sure the club was well compensated financially. Bates moved quickly and decisively to appoint Gary McAllister as Wise's successor—a popular choice among players and fans alike.

When Bates arrived he became Leeds' fifth chairman in 22 months, a remarkable turnover that kept the club very much in the public eye. So what were his predecessors like in their role as chairman?

Gerald Krasner, an expert in insolvency, seemed an ideal figurehead for a club in desperate financial trouble. He and his fellow directors had been supporters of the team but when some of them insisted on visiting the training ground for kick-abouts, their behaviour was frowned upon by the manager at the time Kevin Blackwell and his staff. The club's money problems were so serious that Krasner and his directors resigned in January, 2005, 10 months after taking over and dissolving Leeds United Plc. Krasner went on to become a fierce opponent of Bates' methods and duly became another target for the chairman's barbed comments in the programme!

Not surprisingly, Krasner was not one of Bates's guests in the boardroom when he returned to Elland Road as Bournemouth's administrator in March, 2008. Nor was he given a place in either directors' box. Maybe it was Krasner's brief chairmanship or perhaps it was his lack of charisma that saw not a single autograph hunter approach him when he arrived in the club's main car park before Leeds' match against Bournemouth.

Former Chelsea Chief Executive Trevor Birch had a very brief spell in the chair, following on from Prof. John McKenzie—one of the least likely football club chairmen you could wish to meet. An academic, McKenzie was 65 and the club's second highest individual shareholder with four million shares at the time of his appointment. He was an economist and former head of Ilkley College and it was his thankless task to fill the chair after the free-spending ways of Peter Ridsdale and his board. Although he tried to be media friendly, you gained the impression he was uncomfortable being in the public eye and the Professor lasted less than a year as chairman.

Ridsdale was a different kettle of fish entirely. 'Publicity Pete' had known Don Revie well enough to appreciate the value of publicity and he was ever ready with a quote for the local and national media. It is over five years since he resigned as chairman of Leeds United and Leeds United Plc, yet his name still stirs contrasting emotions among Leeds supporters. Some accept that he was first and foremost a fan who had the club's best interests at heart, living the dream and then the nightmare. Others have nothing but condemnation for the man who needed police protection for himself and his family from his severest critics.

I know him well and accept he made mistakes, but there was no bigger fan of Leeds United than Peter Ridsdale, whose compassion when two Leeds fans were stabbed to death in Istanbul was warmly applauded inside and outside football. At the height of his popularity he was appearing on high profile television programmes like *Question Time* and saying all the right things. Some even likened him to Tony Blair—and just like Blair he fell from grace with an almighty thud.

During Ridsdale's chairmanship Leeds reached the semi-final of the Champions League, visiting some of the top grounds in Europe. The debit side included the club's financial collapse and, through no fault of his own, the Jonathan Woodgate and Lee Bowyer court case. When the ex managing director of Top Man became Leeds United's chairman in 1997, 10 years after joining the board of directors, he could never have envisaged the emotional roller-coaster ride that was to follow. His book, *United We Fall*, attempts to put the record straight on his years at the helm and it is worth recording that the DTI inquiry into the running of Leeds United during his chairmanship cleared all members of the club's Plc of any wrong-doing despite the mistakes which had been made.

Ridsdale's predecessor was the ebullient Bill Fotherby, who had more front than Blackpool promenade. Bill was and still is a larger than life character to whom football is like a drug. As chairman of Harrogate Town he expends as much energy and enthusiasm as he did as Leeds United's commercial director and chairman. He even had a spell as chairman of Rugby League strugglers Hunslet where his commercial expertise was very much to the fore in sealing much needed sponsorship deals.

As I've mentioned elsewhere in this book, Bill was responsible for what I still regard as an outrageous publicity stunt when he telephoned two local evening paper journalists, including myself, to announce Leeds United's interest in signing the infamous 'Hand of God' footballer Maradona. True, he had spoken to the Argentine's agent but that was as far as the story went. Bill was happy with the publicity it generated—front page news—though his haste in going to the press is said to have embarrassed the club's Plc board. Bill relished transfer negotiations and I would love to have been a fly on the wall when he met Eric Hall, the motor-mouthed football agent, to discuss John Scales' transfer from Tottenham to Leeds—another deal that came to nothing. Bill and Eric were two of a kind and, with their patter, what a double act they would have made! When I needed to phone him recently, Bill greeted me like a long lost son, though to this day he gets my name wrong by calling me Ray.

Leeds businessman Leslie Silver was the club's chairman from December, 1983, to April, 1996. Although he resigned through ill health, he still attends home matches and retains a keen interest in the club's affairs. Leslie, who made his money in the paint business after leaving the RAF, was a close friend of Don Revie and no-one was more delighted than Leslie when Howard Wilkinson's team won the League Championship in 1992 for the first time since Revie's era. Silver had been instrumental in appointing Wilkinson and under Leslie's chairmanship the club introduced an identity card scheme to help in the war against the hooligans who had repeatedly dragged Leeds' name through the mud.

Manny Cussins will be remembered as the chairman who sacked manager Brian Clough after just 44 days in the job. Cussins was a self made millionaire who started out by pushing a hand-cart to gather furniture and went on to become head of the John Peters chain. Manny was a workaholic who insisted on visiting his shops to keep his staff on their toes when Leeds United were on their travels. Long after retirement age he could often be found on the shop floor in Leeds making his next sale. Helen and I bought our first suite from him and it wasn't the last, as he talked us into more 'bargain' purchases. I suspect Manny regretted giving Clough the Leeds job within minutes of the former Brighton manager's arrival at Elland Road as Don Revie's successor in 1974. Clough, clearly irritated by the posse of pressmen who followed him into the stadium, rounded on the embarrassed chairman and stormed: 'So this is how you run your club!'

Jimmy Armfield, Jock Stein, Jimmy Adamson, Allan Clarke and Eddie Gray all worked under Cussins' chairmanship but they couldn't win any silverware and the club was relegated to Division Two.

Ald. Percy Woodward, a former Lord Mayor of Leeds, was the club's chairman when I began covering United's affairs for the *Telegraph & Argus* in 1970 and I sat next to him on the flight back from the club's shock fourth round exit from the

FA Cup at Fourth Division Colchester in February, 1971. Turning to me he said in all seriousness that small clubs like Colchester shouldn't be allowed in the competition! United won the Championship under Woodward's chairmanship and took the FA Cup for the first and only time in 1972 with victory over Arsenal at Wembley.

22

THE BUZZ NEVER
LEAVES YOU

When you've covered a team at the top, it's hard watching that team brought to its knees by financial mismanagement. Leeds United very nearly went out of business just a few years after reaching the Champions League semi-final. Fans who had 'lived the dream' by watching their team perform at such illustrious venues as the Nou Camp in Barcelona, the Bernabéu in Madrid and the San Siro in Milan, were suddenly digging out their route maps to Crewe, Gillingham and Stoke. Still worse, following relegation to League One, the fixture list included the 'delights' of Cheltenham, Hartlepool and Yeovil.

The board of directors, under the chairmanship of Peter Ridsdale, spent vast sums in the hope of guaranteeing Champions League fare at Elland Road for years to come. Unfortunately in football there are no guarantees and when Leeds missed out on the Champions League by one place, the pack of cards came tumbling down in spectacular fashion.

Relegation from the Premiership was bad enough, but defeat in a ridiculously one-sided promotion play-off final against Watford was followed by freefall to the lower reaches of the Championship, some embarrassingly heavy defeats, administration and relegation to football's third tier for the first time in the club's history.

Then came the bombshell of that 15 point deduction from the start of the 2007–08 season, imposed by the Football

League for failing to comply with the League's policy for clubs entering administration.

Fortunately, everyone connected with the club—players, management and fans—adopted a siege mentality against the Football League, so incensed were they by what they perceived as a gross miscarriage of justice. A superb run of victories from the season's start wiped out the 15 point deficit in the quickest possible time and Elland Road crowds exceeded many of those in the Premier League, but despite a superb effort the team just missed out on promotion by losing the play-off final to Doncaster.

Before Ken Bates rescued Leeds from potential oblivion, reporters spent more time writing about potential takeovers and mysterious sheikhs than anything else, with football matches almost incidental. It was a crazy time of rumour and counter-rumour. A procession of potential buyers revelled in publicity but failed to come up with sufficient funds as the club lurched from crisis to crisis.

Players, coaches and office staff couldn't be sure of being paid and there was a revolving door of players arriving on loan or being sold to cut the club's crippling debts. Bates became the club's fifth chairman in 22 months and managers had come and gone so rapidly that any chance of continuity was lost.

Then, when the club went into administration after the Inland Revenue ran out of patience, power struggles again hogged the headlines as Leeds faced a potentially damaging transfer embargo. These days, most sports lay out the red carpet for the media. Sadly, football has much catching up to do. Believe it or not, reporters who turned up to cover the creditors' meeting at Elland Road, where a vote was taken on Bates' controversial buy-back from the administrators, had to stand in the street outside the ground's entrance. Banned from attending the meeting, we were reduced to grabbing creditors for snippets of information as they left the ground. Nor were there any press handouts after the meeting. Surely the administrators, or someone connected with the club, could have provided a room and light refreshments for the 20 or so members of the media who were thankful for a dry, sunny day as they waited for hours for the meeting to end. What the publicity-conscious Don Revie would have made of it all I can only imagine.

Not that the media were always treated well in the so-called 'Good Old Days'. I'm reliably informed by one of my seniors that in the far off years when the redoubtable Sam Bolton was Leeds United's chairman and a member of the FA Council, he chaired a long drawn-out board meeting at Elland Road. I believe the subject for discussion was the future of the legendary John Charles. The press were massed outside and, after a seemingly endless wait, there was excitement as Mr Bolton came downstairs as if to address the assembled throng. Sticking out his considerable chest, the gentleman announced: 'I have a statement for you all—no comment.'

When the press persisted in asking questions, Sam told them curtly: 'I've given you a statement. It's "no comment." Isn't that good enough for you?'

For anyone with affection for Leeds United, the last few years have been a time of heartbreak, with standards plummeting. When team sheets were handed to the press before matches I used them to check the identity of opposition players. Nowadays I struggle to identify Leeds United's players as so many of them have flitted in and out of Elland Road.

For pressmen who have followed the club through the good times and relished their trips into Europe, it has been a similarly hard blow—especially for those unable or unwilling to hook on to another bandwagon in a different town or city. How can covering Leeds United against Hartlepool, for instance, compare with Leeds against Real Madrid? Yet despite it all, I still get a buzz every time I park the car at

Elland Road and make my way to the press room in readiness for another home game. Reporting from the press box is like a drug—you may not always like what you see unfolding in front of your eyes on that pitch, but you need it and can't give it up.

No matter how good or bad a match may be there's always a story to tell and the newspapers are there to tell it. With websites, TV and radio stations providing blanket coverage, the demise of the printed word has long been predicted. Yet newspapers remain one of the most popular sources of sporting information. They've had to adapt, of course, by interpreting the news through feature articles because other branches of the media are more immediate. The battle is still being fought against falling circulations and diminishing advertising revenue, but fortunately there are enough newspaper owners willing to ride out the hard times.

Sadly, most Saturday night sports papers have ceased publication. It is often said that you don't appreciate something until it has gone. That is certainly true of our much lamented Saturday sports papers. So many of them became victims of falling readership and an eagerness by newsagents to shut up shop when Saturday teatime came around. Nor were matters helped by a minority of on-street newspaper sellers who seized the opportunity to abscond with the proceeds!

It hasn't been easy for publishers setting up new titles, either. One of the newspapers launched with considerable optimism was *Yorkshire On Sunday*, produced in the Bradford *Telegraph & Argus* building. It was generally acknowledged as an excellent paper—especially the sports pages which gave the kind of coverage to sport in the county which the national Sundays couldn't match. In its short life it provided Gosnay's with welcome income from football, cricket and rugby coverage. Unfortunately, the paper didn't make enough money and it lasted just three years in the early to mid nineties. In my opinion it wasn't marketed sufficiently. In fact, many of my friends didn't even know it existed.

Perhaps if TV, websites and local radio stations did a less efficient job, many now defunct papers would still be on the streets, and if newsagents could be persuaded to stay open longer on Saturday nights, our sports papers may still be thriving. I also have to say that if everyone who now bemoans the passing of the pinks and greens had bought a copy every week, whether their team had won or lost, it would have helped.

It's sad to think of a whole generation of sports fans denied that glowing feeling on Saturday teatime when their team had slaughtered the opposition and every move was described in detail by their favourite sports paper. For the sportswriter, too, there was the satisfying challenge of filing several hundred words to his office every 15 minutes or so, while attempting to keep a watchful eye on the play. There were problems with telephones which refused to work, problems hearing copy-takers above the din of the crowd and occasionally problems identifying players shrouded in fog or caked in mud.

Pity the poor sub-editor whose carefully thought-out, punchy headline had to be hastily re-written because Billy Bremner, for instance, had popped up with an injury-time goal to transform the result. Yet I wouldn't have missed the excitement of those hectic Saturday afternoons for a fortune.

Can you really imagine life without our national and regional papers and the journalists who write them? I hope not. Since so many national newspapers closed their northern offices, the number of editions has been cut considerably, enabling the publishers to reduce their staffs and save on wages. When new technology was on its way, evening paper journalists were assured it would bring opportunities for even more editions and news updates throughout the day. In practice, most evening papers have reduced their editions drastically and some have removed the word 'Evening' from their title. Papers are on the streets much earlier in the day but anyone wanting bang up to date news stories has to rely on television and radio news bulletins or websites. Ironically, you can read many stories on newspaper websites before they appear in print! And they wonder why circulations continue to fall.

For me, covering Leeds United has been a long roller-coaster ride. There have been highs, like the FA Cup triumph in 1972, the European Cup semi-final knockout of Barcelona in 1975, the League Championship successes in 1974 and 1992, promotion from the old second division in 1990, the march to the Champions League semi-final in 2001. And there was that tremendous start to the 2007–08 season in League One when the 15 point deficit was rapidly wiped out. There are also encouraging signs after the early weeks of the 2008–09 campaign that manager Gary McAllister has what it takes to drive the club forward.

Then there have been the lows like that humbling FA Cup defeat at Colchester in 1971, the FA Cup final heartbreak against Sunderland in 1973, the Coca-Cola League Cup final defeat against Aston Villa in 1996, European Cup final disappointment against Bayern Munich in 1975, relegation from the top flight in 1982 and 2004, defeat to Watford in the 2006 promotion play-off final, relegation from the Championship. Just a year later came more disappointment with that defeat to Doncaster in the League One play-off final at the new Wembley.

The trip to Cardiff's Millennium Stadium for the Championship promotion play-off was a nightmare for several reasons. It should have been a thoroughly enjoyable experience. For the first time in many years I teamed up with my old mates Don Warters and Barry Foster for the car journey to South Wales and all was going well as we arrived in good time at the NCP car park next to the ground.

Yet, after an appetising meal in the media centre and an appreciation of the Millennium Stadium's state of the art facilities, the day went rapidly downhill. Watford, managed by former Leeds coach Adrian Boothroyd, were in a different class as they swept to a 3–0 victory that could have been even more comprehensive. It left Leeds fans totally disillusioned and proved the prelude to a season of turmoil as the side battled for Championship survival. The *Daily Sport* had ordered a match follow-up piece from me and, after collecting quotes from the major characters of the drama, I returned to the media centre where my laptop ran out of battery life just as I was about to send several hundred words by e-mail.

No problem, I thought. I'll plug my AC adaptor into one of the many electrical points provided. Unfortunately, the adaptor had developed an untimely fault and refused to charge up the laptop, so I had no access to the story I had carefully prepared. Fellow journalists offered to loan me their adaptors but why, oh why, are these peripherals not manufactured to standard proportions? None of the adaptors would fit into my laptop and so much time had passed that starting my story again and reciting it to a copy-taker was no longer practical. The guys at the *Daily Sport* were remarkably understanding in the circumstances and, as most of the quotes I had gleaned were exclusive, they didn't date.

So with the story slightly amended, it duly appeared in the *Daily Sport* a day later than intended. Unfortunately, the press room drama had delayed our return to the car park and when we arrived at the NCP we found the entrance locked up, with my car inside. There were visions of having to book into a hotel and spend the night in Cardiff until I found a telephone number to ring and an NCP employee kindly agreed to make a 20 minute journey so he could release my car. We were so grateful to him that we insisted on handing over the sandwiches and drinks we had been given in the media centre for the journey home.

Despite the long delay at the stadium, we were caught up in an horrendous traffic jam out of Cardiff which delayed us for at least another hour. They say the food at motorway service stations isn't the best, but by the time we reached the M6 we were so ravenous that it was a case of any port in a storm. The café area had finished serving, a burger bar was about to close and we were just in time to order the last three burgers remaining.

Under normal circumstances I would have complained that my burger was cold, but as the shutters had come down and the staff were obviously preparing to leave, I just cursed under my breath and ate the excuse for a meal. Arriving back in Leeds late at night I offered up a prayer of thanks that travelling hundreds of miles to report on football matches is a rarity for me these days.

Despite my fall-out with Brian Clough all those years ago, I am happy to say I've made far more friends in sport than enemies—and I can't imagine life without press boxes, training grounds, laptop computers, telephones and the countless characters I've transported from pitch to page. Sports journalism can be exhilarating, frustrating, rewarding and challenging. Its time consuming nature is enough to put any marriage to the severest of tests and many is the time I've thanked God for having a wife as understanding as Helen. Fortunately, I've never had a job which has taken me away from home for longer than a week or so at a time. How the marriages of journalists who spend half their lives travelling the world survive I can't imagine.

Would I go into sports journalism again if I was just starting out on the career ladder? Probably. Yet the job has changed in so many ways. Every generation thinks it has lived through the best years and I will always be thankful for hitching a ride on the back of Leeds United's glory years before my city club's spectacular fall from grace.

It's a wonderful life when laptops work as they should do, stories receive the coverage they deserve and the cheques come in on time. And it's even better when the team you've covered for so many years actually wins! It alarms me when I come across young journalists who are taught to quote players and managers verbatim. If you've ever sat in on a press conference, you'll appreciate that those sitting behind the table, with some exceptions, murder the English language.

Journalists do them a favour by putting their comments into decent English, while keeping to the point of their message. If we quoted them verbatim they would sound ridiculous. So please, journalism course tutors, don't tell your pupils to quote people word for word. It only makes extra work for the sub-editor.

Finally, my favourite story about a member of the media doesn't involve a newspaper at all. My old friend John Helm, a renowned TV commentator, was covering a match in Goa, India, where officials were keen to raise the profile of the country's football. Goa had the most prolific forward in the country, so John was looking to feature him heavily in his commentary.

Unfortunately, when the team sheet arrived, the star's name was absent. On asking the reason, John was told in broken English: 'Ah sir, he had very bad accident. He bitten by dog with rabies.'

John expressed his concern and asked after the player's welfare. Back came the perfectly serious reply: 'Ah sir, him alive; dog dead.'